The New York Times

CHANGING PERSPECTIVES

Medical Treatments

THE NEW YORK TIMES EDITORIAL STAFF

Published in 2020 by New York Times Educational Publishing
in association with The Rosen Publishing Group, Inc.
29 East 21st Street, New York, NY 10010

First Edition

The New York Times
Alex Ward: Editorial Director, Book Development
Phyllis Collazo: Photo Rights/Permissions Editor
Heidi Giovine: Administrative Manager

Rosen Publishing
Megan Kellerman: Managing Editor
Xina M. Uhl: Editor
Greg Tucker: Creative Director
Brian Garvey: Art Director

Cataloging-in-Publication Data
Names: New York Times Company.
Title: Medical treatments / edited by the New York Times editorial staff.
Description: New York : New York Times Educational Publishing,
2020. | Series: Changing perspectives | Includes glossary and index.
Identifiers: ISBN 9781642822304 (library bound) | ISBN
9781642822298 (pbk.) | ISBN 9781642822311 (ebook)
Subjects: LCSH: Medical technology—Juvenile literature. |
Medical innovations—Juvenile literature.
Classification: LCC R855.4 M435 2020 | DDC 610.1'4—dc23

Manufactured in the United States of America

On the cover: A surgeon and his team perform key hole surgery to
remove a gallbladder at Queen Elizabeth Hospital Birmingham in
England; Christopher Furlong/Getty Images.

Contents

CHAPTER 4

New Diseases and New Fixes for Old Ones: 1960–1999

CHAPTER 5

Treatments Never Before Seen: 2000–Present

Introduction

UNTIL THE MID-NINETEENTH century, medicine had limited success in treating mankind's many ills. Poor sanitation, crowded living conditions and malnutrition conspired to spread a host of diseases. The lack of pain control and safe surgical methods made surgeries to repair injuries or remove infected tissues an almost-certain prescription for death. Yet a golden age in medicine soon dawned. Scientists such as Louis Pasteur, and doctors like Joseph Lister and Robert Koch, made startling advances in germ theory. Germ theory revealed that microorganisms in the body cause many diseases. From this basis sprang a host of positive results.

Researchers worked steadily to develop vaccines to target specific diseases like diphtheria, cholera and tuberculosis. Widespread public acceptance of vaccines followed these discoveries. Standard cleanliness by doctors and nurses was not practiced until this period. Operating rooms lacked masks and head coverings, doctors often did not bother changing their clothing from surgery to surgery, and medical instruments were not sterilized. New procedures that required cleanliness changed all that.

Antiseptics, which work by slowing or stopping the growth of germs, come in two types. One type involves various chemicals that destroy germs. These chemicals are applied to all surfaces and items used in surgeries. A second type of antiseptic is called antibiotics. They are medicines taken internally by patients to fight harmful germs within the body.

Anesthesia refers to certain drugs that cause loss of feeling in patients. Prior to their discovery in the late 1800s, most patients died from shock during surgeries. With the use of anesthesia, patients are free of pain and unconscious during surgeons' delicate operations.

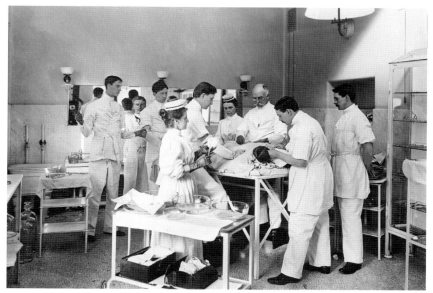

Medical treatments have evolved by leaps and bounds in the past two centuries. Seen here third from right, Dr. Charles McBurney (1845–1913), famous for his discovery of the "McBurney Point" as a sign for operative intervention in appendicitis, operates in Roosevelt Hospital, New York, 1901.

Germ theory, combined with vaccines and efforts by cities to clean up water and sewage, caused a golden era of increased health. Life expectancy skyrocketed into the early twentieth century, from a mere forty years in 1800 to sixty years by 1930.

Researchers continued to tackle one disease after another through the use of new vaccines and the worldwide acceptance of them, leading to the complete eradication of smallpox, a once deadly and disfiguring ailment. The most important of these was the discovery of antibiotics such as penicillin. Suddenly, infectious diseases like pneumonia did not have to result in death. The discovery of vitamins' effect on health, and the development of medical devices such as X-rays that allow doctors to see within human bodies and make accurate diagnoses, are just two of many other significant medical advancements.

As time passed and refinements in procedures, science and technology continued, new diseases also arose. One of the most significant of these was HIV, a devastating virus that, if left untreated, leads to AIDS and a difficult death.

Modern-day challenges often involve ethics and morals. Medical marijuana uses have been growing in popularity despite decades-long restrictions on the use of the drug. Cloning raises concerns on the world stage that humans may be created without rights and with significant health problems from the procedure. Science's triumph in discovering DNA and mapping the human genome has created a new level of sophistication in dealing with medical concerns. Robots and artificial intelligence are continuing to develop and serve as surgical tools as well as new prosthetics for missing limbs.

Many illnesses, conditions and injuries that once seemed impossible to cope with are now commonly treated by medical professionals the world over, and what is revolutionary one day may become routine the next. As the articles in this collection reveal, the range of medical treatments developed since the inception of The New York Times is not only impressive, but important to understand as humanity continues to develop and prosper.

CHAPTER 1

Anesthesia, Antiseptics and Vaccines: 1851–1899

Before the age of anesthesia and antiseptics, surgery was an agonizing, deadly proposition. The development of a safe means of making a patient unconscious and free of pain during surgical procedures made it possible for surgeons to repair severed limbs and infected organs, and even remove tumors. Antiseptics kept surgeons from introducing bacteria into patients' bodies during surgery. The discovery and use of vaccines had a profound effect on a multitude of lethal illnesses, including rabies, yellow fever, cholera, diphtheria and consumption (also known as tuberculosis). Other advances included embalming, blood transfusions and the discovery of X-rays.

Medical.

BY THE NEW YORK TIMES | MARCH 17, 1854

A PARISIAN CORRESPONDENT of the *Medical Times* (Dr. W. E. Johnston,) narrates two extraordinary surgical operations. The first was a Dr. J., who, by carelessly holding in his mouth glass tubes charged with vaccine matter, contracted an "Epithelial Cancrord" induration, which, in spite of internal medication and external cauterization, rapidly so spread itself that it was deemed necessary to amputate. The patient was put under the influence of chloroform. M. Maisonneuve cut through the soft parts of the lower lip to the chin, and with a chain saw divided the lower maxillary bone. The section of the chin was then drawn apart, which enabled the surgeon to seize the tongue and draw it well out of the mouth. By a rapid dissection, the diseased organ was separated from the healthy parts, at a point beyond the anterior half, an extent of eight centimetres — a little over three inches. The sublingual gland was sacrificed; ligatures were applied to the important vessels, and no hemorrhage followed. After the operation, the branches of the separated jaw were brought into apposition, and secured by threads passed around the teeth. The ligatures placed on the vessels were brought out, under the edge of the jaw, at the lower angle of the wound; and the borders of the division were united by the twisted suture. Notwithstanding the extreme gravity of this operation, no unpleasant results followed. The external parts cicatrized by first intention, the bones consolidated, the enormous loss of substance filled up rapidly, and what is remarkable, *the patient has recovered his speech*, as well as the power of seizing and masticating his food! The other was to relieve a man who suffered from a bony tumor arising from the internal angles of the orbit of the eye, and occupying nearly the whole orbit. The soft parts were so dissected that the eye hung entirely out of the orbit, and on the cheek. By virtue of a cold chisel, mallet, levers manifold and a crow, the whole bony tumor was chipped out, the eye replaced, and without any trouble at all, the operation was so successful that a month after it was difficult to say on which eye the operation had been performed.

Prof. Brainard, of Chicago, is in Paris, although expecting soon to return to the United States. He presented to the Academy of Sciences a paper on the bite of a rattlesnake. His treatment is — apply a cupping glass over the bitten part, thrust a small trocar to which a syringe is attached beneath the skin and under the edge of the cup, and then inject half a drachm or more of a solution of 5 grains of iodine with 15 grains of iodide of potassium, to the ounce of water. The cup is allowed to remain on some 5 minutes. This treatment has worked well on the birds, kittens, and pups, that he experimented with. It would do well he thinks in case of dissection, wounds, &c. Dr. B. has in press a volume on *Pseudarthrosis* and the use of the Seton in ununitted fractures. He dissents from the usual practice in such cases.

Modern Embalming.

FROM THE CORRESPONDENT OF THE NEWARK ADVERTISER | APRIL 20, 1855

I HAVE LATELY WITNESSED the process of embalming as practised here. It was on the person of a young American, whose friends wished the body preserved as perfectly as possible, in order to its being sent home. The law requires that 24 hours' notice of the decease shall be given to the police by the attending physician, before either autopsy or embalming shall be practised. The design of the regulation is to give certainty that death has really taken place, and in a legitimate manner. Embalmers are prohibited from employing arsenic, an excellent antiseptic, because in cases of death from that poison administered wilfully, their use of it would defeat the ends of justice. The mode of procedure in this instance was as follows: The operator first filled two vials with his preparation, and gave them to a police officer who was present, to be sealed and subsequently analyzed by a competent chemist. If the least trace of the prohibited article should be found, the embalmer would be liable to severe punishment. He then, through the carotid artery and by means of a large syringe, furnished with a detached stopcock, injected about a gallon of a reddish fluid which, I have since learned, had probably chloride of zinc for its base. As the vessels became distended, this fluid permeated the capillaries, marking its passage by arborescent white lines, until gradually a considerable portion of the skin assumed a clear pearly lustre, which I was informed would after a time be the case with the whole surface. The body then, after being washed in Cologne water, having the nostrils and ears stuffed with cotton dipped in some extract of a musky odor, the cheeks and lips painted, the eyeballs fitted with glass fronts of the natural shade, and the hands and feet clad in silk gloves and stockings, was surrounded with four coffins, the inner shell being lined with lead, and the outer one leaving the appearance of a box containing goods. And so our poor friend was transported to his mourning relatives. The same steamer that carried this, took out also two other American corpses.

Simple as is the process of embalming, it is very costly. For that and the four coffins, I believe the demand was two thousand francs. In reply to some questions as to the efficacy of his process, the embalmer declared that he had known bodies preserved by it perfectly during five years, and he thought the time of its action might he extended greatly beyond that limit.

Substitute for Anesthesia.

BY THE NEW YORK TIMES | JAN. 4, 1860

The Boston Traveller publishes the following: Rue De La Chausse D'antin, Paris, Monday, Dec. 12, 1859.

I CANNOT LET this steamship leave here and not acquaint you with one of the most extraordinary discoveries recently made. Monsieur Velpeau, the eminent surgeon, whose fame is wide as the world, made the strange communication. He stated that an honorable surgeon or physician (he vouched for the gentleman's character,) named Brocca or Rocca, had made the following experiment: He had placed before the face of a person, between the person's eyes, and at a distance of fifteen or twenty *centimetres* (a *centimetre* is a French measure of length — 0393.708 inch in value) a rather brilliant object (*un objet un peu brillant*). Make the person look fixedly at this object. In a few minutes the person will squint, and will soon fall into catalepsy and be spontaneously deprived of all sensibility.

In the experiments made, the insensibility of the patient was so great that the patient's head was alternately moved from one side to the other, and his whole person was moved. He had no recollection of any of them when he returned to his normal state.

This singular discovery made Mons. Rocca or Brocca suspect that this state of insensibility might be as perfect as that obtained by anesthetic agents. He determined to make experiments with it, and found that the state of insensibility produced was as perfect as that obtained by the use of ether and chloroform.

Three experiments out of five attempts are reported as successful. In one of these cases a man underwent a surgical operation for an abscess, which required an important incision. The insensibility lasted ten or fifteen minutes after the operation. The patient was entirely unconscious of all that had taken place.

The experiments mentioned by Mons. Velpeau may be easily repeated by anybody. Their importance in point of economy and money and life is serious. Chloroform and ether are both costly articles, and their use is attended with danger. They have destroyed more than one life, and medical men are still unable to vaticinate in what states of the body they may be used innocuously, and when they will extinguish life. Besides, their use in the lesser surgical operations, such as the extraction of teeth, is generally considered, out of the City of Boston, to be eminently injudicious. What a blessing this new discovery will prove, if time and experiment avouch all its present advantages.

Mons. Velpeau, in announcing the new discovery, said: "It is a strange phenomenon, so strange a phenomenon that I feel obliged to take some oratorical precautions in speaking of it to the Academy of Sciences. I feel obliged to draw assurance from the talents and honorable character of Mons. Brocca, who has charged me with the duty of giving his discovery useful publicity, and at the same time of assuring his right to the discovery of this remarkable phenomenon."

Mons. Velpeau, therefore, does not present the new system of anesthesia for a panacea, but he says to medical men: "Use it, study it, experiment on it on useful occasions, and perhaps you may contribute to endow science with a new means of alleviating suffering humanity."

A New Anaesthetic Process.

BY THE NEW YORK TIMES | APRIL 1, 1866

A NEW PROCESS for producing what is technically called "local anaesthesia," but which we know by the humbler and less jaw-breaking name of "a deadened sensation," has been discovered and brought into practice by Dr. Richardson. It consists in directing on the part of the body to be operated upon perfectly pure ether in the form of infinitely minute subdivision of fine spray. The instrument invented by Dr. Richardson for this purpose consists of a dispersion tube connected with a small hand bellows, and fixed in a bottle of ether. When the bellows are brought into action the ether is delivered from a capillary jet, and is directed to the body at a distance of from half an inch to an inch and a half. In a very brief period, varying according to the circulatory power of the patient from five to fifty seconds, the portion of the body under the influence of the ether spray becomes of snowy whiteness, and absolutely insensible to pain. The skin may now be divided, and the ether being directed into the wound, deeper incisions may be carried on. In a case of disease affecting the thigh in a patient at the great Northern Hospital, Mr. W. Adams, one of the surgeons to the hospital, made an incision five inches long and one inch and a half deep, after Dr. Richardson had thus rendered the parts insensible, and the patient was not even conscious that the knife had been used. Up to the present time, we are informed, Dr. Richardson has applied the local anaesthetic in more than fifty operations, and in all with perfect success. The process has also been adopted with equal success by other practitioners. As yet it has been used only in minor operations, but the author of the plan is of opinion that with a larger and improved apparatus he can make it applicable for capital operations. The principle of the process consists in a combination of a mode of producing sudden and extreme cold by and in combination with an anaesthetic fluid, viz.: ether. The extreme cold causes the superficial numbness of the skin, but when the skin is divided the other exerts its own direct action on the nerves, combined with the action of cold; hence the deep insensibility that results. After the application, the parts quickly recover their sensibility and heal well. The advantages of this method are its great simplicity of application, its rapidity of action, its absolute safety, and its powers as an anaesthetic. The process does not interfere in the least degree with the consciousness, and a very little practice with it makes every surgeon master of the necessary details for its successful employment. The number of deaths that have recently occurred from chloroform have made professional men peculiarly anxious in respect to its use in small operations; while at the same time they have been desirous of operating without, in every case, the production of pain from the knife, Dr. Richardson's discovery is received, therefore, by the profession with a degree of enthusiasm which has probably only once been expressed since the news first came from America of the discovery of general anaesthesia by the inhalation of vapor. We mean when Professor, now Sir James Simpson, announced the discovery of chloroform as the substitute for ether.

Horace Wells.

BY THE NEW YORK TIMES | MAY 23, 1873

IF WE ARE TO CREDIT the unanimous testimony of the three eminent physicians who on Wednesday evening, at Steinway Hall, illustrated the history of anaesthesia, the memory of Horace Wells should be revered as that of a chief benefactor of the human race. To the young Hartford dentist, these gentlemen assure us, is to be assigned all the honor for a discovery whose value to mankind is hardly to be overestimated. Morton and Jackson discovered that sulphuric ether was an anaesthetic; Warren revealed the similar properties of chloric ether; Sir James Y. Simpson gave chloroform to science, and Richardson first found out the pain-subduing virtues of bichloride of mythelene. But Horace Wells first discovered and applied the great principle of anaesthesia which led the way to all these other discoveries. Yet Horace Wells died not only poor and unhonored, like many another inventor before him, but absolutely driven mad by unmerited neglect and obloquy. Others in his lifetime reaped the substantial benefits of his great discovery, and still after his death do wrong to his memory by usurping the fame that should be his.

The first of these injuries is irreparable. The second can still be repaired. It has been said satirically that Americans have two ways of honoring their distinguished man. If he is alive they give him a dinner. If he is dead they collect money to build him a monument, which they forget to build. If we suggest that Americans owe a monument to the discoverer of anaesthesia, it is with the hope of falsifying a part at least of the satire. On many grounds Horace Wells seems to deserve this poor atonement from his countrymen, not least because, the master of a secret that was worth a fortune, he chose rather to make it a free gift to humanity than to hoard it for his private emolument. Such men are rare, and their names should be proportionately honored. A statue in Central Park would not be much to do for one who has done so much for human happiness, and the greatest of those whose images adorn its drives would be the first, we may be sure, to welcome the company of the poor, unfriended, and well-nigh forgotten dentist. Why do not the gentlemen who have already done so much to make known the claims of Horace Wells to the community, take the further task in hand of securing some lasting and adequate memorial of his services?

In Pasteur's Laboratory

BY COMMERCIAL CABLE FROM OUR OWN CORRESPONDENT | DEC. 22, 1885

PARIS, DEC. 21. — The steamship Canada, which sailed from New-York on Dec. 9 for Havre, having on board Patrick Reynolds, Willie Lane, Patrick Ryan, and Austin Fitzgerald, the Newark boys who had been bitten by a mad dog, arrived off Havre last night, but was unable to enter the harbor until this morning. The correspondent of The Times was at the dock when the Canada reached it and was warmly greeted by Dr. Billings, who gave him the details of the voyage. There was no incident worthy of particular note. The trip was an easy one and the children behaved well. Young Reynolds, who was full of a boy's animal spirits, was at times a terror to the servants and sailors, who mistook his monkey pranks for indications of the development of hydrophobia. The debarkation was a tedious affair, but the party finally started in a special train for Paris, and arrived here at 3 o'clock in the afternoon. Mrs. Ryan and the children under her charge were placed in comfort in a small hotel near M. Pasteur's laboratory. Dr. Billings, guided by The Times's correspondent, then started in search of M. Pasteur. It was now 5 o'clock, and little hope was entertained of finding the object of search, but fortunately the precaution had been taken to inform him by telegraph of the coming of the party, and he was found waiting in his office in the Normal School, Rue Ulm. M. Pasteur welcomed Dr. Billings most cordially and suggested that the inoculation be made tomorrow.

"But cannot it be attended to to-night?" asked Dr. Billings.

"Certainly, if you insist upon it," replied M. Pasteur.

"The sooner the better," explained Dr. Billings.

M. Pasteur then said: "My medical assistant has gone home for the night. Will you make the injection?"

"I would do so most willingly," Dr. Billings replied, "were it not so much better to have it done by a resident physician."

Louis Pasteur.

"Very well, then," rejoined M. Pasteur, "I will send for Dr. Grancher, my assistant, and ask him to come this evening. If he can come I will gladly inoculate the children to-night. Return to your hotel and wait."

Scarcely had the soup with which the dinner was begun been finished when word was brought that M. Pasteur and assistant would be ready for the party at 7 o'clock. It is scarcely necessary to say that we were punctual. In the laboratory were at the hour gathered all the members of the party, including Mrs. Ryan. We had to wait a few minutes while M. Pasteur inoculated a Hungarian officer, who had been bitten a fortnight before at Pesth by the mad dog of a druggist. This officer, who is a handsome fellow, had been badly bitten in his right arm. When he came out of the laboratory Dr. Grancher produced a vial of virus, syringes, and lancets.

"Begin with the eldest first," directed M. Pasteur, whereupon the youngest at once began to bawl, but was soon quieted. Young was chosen as the first subject, seated in a chair, and told to uncover his abdomen. M. Pasteur was seated close to the boy on the right and Dr. Grancher in front. The latter filled his syringe, gathered up a portion of the flesh near the navel, and before the boy fairly realized what was happening, had thrust in the instrument and the inoculation was safely over. The turns of Fitzgerald, Reynolds, and Baby Ryan then followed. Each of the children bore the operation bravely. The whole affair lasted less than a quarter of an hour. M. Pasteur did not look at the wounds, but he was full of gentleness and sympathy for the children.

At Dr. Billings's request the savant was informed that the doctor had six dogs locked up which had been bitten by the animal from whose mad fury the children were sufferers.

"Kill them! Kill them!"he said, with great emphasis.

"But," said Dr. Billings, "I want to keep them and see if they will go mad. The result will test the value of your operation in the case of these children."

"Ah, very good! Excellent!" responded M. Pasteur.

Dr. Billings asked permission to visit other parts of the laboratory, and M. Pasteur replied: "Yes, you shall see all to-morrow. I will show you everything. I will take you to see my dogs, and give you some virus to take to America."

When asked how many cases like these he had had, he replied: "Let me see; these make 114 since the beginning." "How many cases have you now under your charge?"

"About 20, and all are doing well."

When asked: "How long do you want us to stay in Paris," he replied: "I will be glad if you remain at least eight or ten days. Drive the boys around here in the morning, so that I can look at them and tell when they will require another injection."

Thus we left him. The children are now sleeping peacefully, in apparent contentment and good health.

Vaccination Against Cholera.

BY THE NEW YORK TIMES | MAY 9, 1893

DR. HAFFKINE OF THE Pasteur Institute has an article in the *Fortnightly Review* giving the results of the investigations upon the subject of vaccination against cholera. He describes minutely the series of inquiries which resulted in his obtaining the material which he uses as vaccine. The writer indeed does not touch upon one point. Cholera does not belong to that type of infectious diseases in which one attack gives subsequent immunity, and this fact would appear to offer a serious obstacle to its prevention or control by any form of vaccination.

It was only after many experiments had been made on animals of widely different species, demonstrating the perfect harmlessness of the process and its absolute efficaciousness, that it was tried on human beings. Dr. Haffkine wished to be the first object of the experiment, but another enthusiast of science, Mr. Vilbonche-Vitch, insisted the experiment should be first tried on him. The vaccination was performed also on forty other persons. In some of these operations Dr. Haffkine modified the process by using vaccines preserved in phenic acid, instead of living vaccines. It was found that the dead vaccines served the purpose just as well as the living ones. These microbes act by means of the substances they create. They quickly perish as soon as they are introduced into the body of the subject, as has been demonstrated in the case of the experiments on guinea pigs. The little parasite may as well, therefore, be killed before injection, for the substances contained in its corpse will still exercise a very powerful effect. But the dead vaccines have many advantages over the living ones. They may be handled with absolute security, and they may be trusted to an unskilled operator. The fact that they are dead allows of their preservation for any period of time.

Whether the vaccines be dead or living, the symptoms felt by the vaccinated persons are about the same — a headache, a little fever, and a dull pain at the place of inoculation. Prof. Gessard of Val de Grâce, one of the first persons to be inoculated, says that the symptoms are no worse than those of a strong cold in the head or a slight touch of influenza. These symptoms usually disappear in twenty-four hours. There remains only a sensitiveness and a hardening of the skin, which, however, disappears in three to five days. There have been about 100 injections performed on human beings with perfectly harmless results. In the numerous experiments which Dr. Haffkine made on animals, not one has been lost. These facts seem to show the harmlessness of the operation.

There is no difficulty in demonstrating its efficaciousness in the case of any animal. The custom is to take ten rabbits, guinea pigs, or pigeons, and to inoculate five of them with the process in question, and to leave the other five in their original condition. Afterward, a sufficient dose of the virus is injected into these animals. The five inoculated animals hardly suffer at all, the five others die eight days afterward, with symptoms characteristic of the infection. A large number of the operations have been performed on animals, always with the same success.

It is obvious that the experiment cannot be performed upon men. If an experiment could be made upon them similar to the famous one of Pasteur in 1881 in vaccinating sheep against anthrax, we should be able to have an immediate solution of the question of efficacy of cholera vaccination. Pasteur vaccinated twenty-five sheep, and twenty-five other sheep were kept as "witnesses." Twelve days afterward the fifty animals were inoculated with the deadly virus of anthrax. The twenty-five vaccinated sheep did not suffer, while the twenty-five "witnesses" died within forty-eight hours. Men, of course, cannot be made "witnesses" of. In the eighteenth century such experiments were made upon persons condemned to death, but they would not be possible in this age. Strange to say, however, there are persons who are willing to act in the capacity of "witnesses." Dr. Haffkine has received such proposals and mentions the case of one French doctor who offered himself as a subject of inoculation — of course, understanding that he was going to almost certain death. When Dr. Haffkine represented that he might be held judicially responsible for his death, he said: "I know how to go about the business; I am myself a doctor; you need only mislay a syringe full of virus in your laboratory."

It may be objected that, although the vaccination may work perfectly well within rabbits and pigeons, it may not work with men. And Dr. Haffkine admits that this is not impossible. But he considers it far from probable. A mammiferous rodent, such as a rabbit or a guinea pig, is, from an anatomical or physiological point of view, much more unlike a bird, such as a pigeon, than it is unlike a man. Furthermore, the symptoms of the vaccination are very similar in the case of all animals, and, this similarity, of course, applies to men. The experiments in the case of Mr. Stanhope, who went to Hamburg after having been inoculated, and of M. Badaire, who swallowed, in the presence of the Paris doctors, a choleraic draught, prepared expressly for him, are, of course, not conclusive. But Dr. Haffkine hopes that the experiment may he tried on a scale large enough to demonstrate its value in some of those Eastern countries where cholera is a permanent disease.

Anti-Toxine Distributed

BY THE NEW YORK TIMES | NOV. 26, 1894

THE FIRST TRADE importation of Behring's diphtheria anti-toxine, the newly-discovered specific for diphtheria, was received in this city late Saturday evening.

The firm first in the field with a supply of what, by some eminent physicians is regarded as a positive cure for diphtheria, is Lehn & Fink, 128 William Street.

Physicians were by them promptly notified of the arrival of the serum, and a representative of the firm was on hand all day Sunday answering inquiries and supplying the diphtheria remedy.

The anti-toxine was only given to physicians who showed proofs of having actual and urgent cases of diphtheria under treatment, these measures being necessitated by the scarcity of the remedy. Its therapeutic value and the opportunities for saving life make it necessary to keep the remedy out of the hands of persons actuated by curiosity or greed.

Among the physicians who obtained supplies for use in their private practice were Prof. August Caillé of the New-York Post-Graduate School and Hospital, 185 Second Avenue, Dr. Seneca D. Powell of 12 West Fortieth Street, Dr. Carl Mund of 308 East Sixty-seventh Street, Dr. Hoenning of Hoboken, N. J., and Dr. Marcus K. Goldsmith of 1,704 Lexington Avenue.

The diphtheria anti-toxine solution, as discovered by Prof. Behring of Berlin, is supplied in three strengths, designated Nos. 1, 2, and 3. The No. 1 is used in the treatment of diphtheria in children under ten years of age, and for all incipient cases. Nos. 2 and 3 are recommended for use in advanced cases.

The injections are made with either a Koch or a Pasteur syringe, and under the ribs, in the loins, or the inner surface of the thighs.

The anti-toxine comes in small bottles, holding ten cubic centimeters — about two teaspoonfuls. The amount contained in each bottle is equivalent to what is termed 600 anti-toxine normals, and is sufficient for one case. No. 2 contains the equivalent of 1,000 anti-toxine normals.

As a prophylactic to persons exposed to diphtheria, it is recommended to inject about sixty anti-toxine normals, or one-tenth of the contents of a vial of No. 1.

To a reporter of The New-York Times, L. F. Fink of the firm said he was much gratified with the response which physicians had made to his invitation to call for supplies of the remedy, and he was well satisfied with the result of his Sunday's work.

Lehn & Fink, in contracting for its distribution, waived all commercial considerations, and a merely nominal price was asked for the seven vials; all of which were quickly disposed of.

So highly is the remedy regarded in Germany that public collections are made through the press for the purpose of buying the anti-toxine and supplying the remedy free for the treatment of the poor.

Dr. Seneca D. Powell, who retires to-night as President of the Medical Society of the County of New-York, said of his purchase and the remedy:

> My attention was called to a letter from Lehn & Fink stating that they had just received by steamer a very limited amount of anti-toxine, which they wished to offer to reputable members of the medical profession for immediate use.
>
> I called and found Mr. Fink, who supplied me with a bottle of Strength No. 1 at a nominal cost. The fact that this firm has placed at the disposition of the medical profession serum that it had procured at great expense and with great difficulty is of considerable importance. I think it merits recognition.
>
> Let me tell you why. The only other anti-toxine that I know of is for sale at $50 a dose.
>
> Do I believe in it? Only by what I have been told by men in whom I have confidence as a result of their experience.
>
> I am just now sending the serum I procured by special post delivery to a prominent physician of Louisville, Ky., who was matriculated at the Post-Graduate here. He telegraphed me yesterday: 'My child has diphtheria; send anti-toxine at any cost.' He not long ago said that diphtheria

was all around him, and he feared his children would catch it. He then knew that anti-toxine could be bought for $50 a dose and asked me about it. I said that any person who would be robber enough to ask such a sum would be dishonest enough to sell a spurious or a diluted serum.

I was again told to-day that there was a supply of the material in the market — not that at Lehn & Fink's — at $50 the dose and that it was furnished by a physician as a speculation. I am ashamed that any man having right to the title of physician should be guilty of such vile, unprofessional greed of gain. I cannot give his name, but it will be divulged in the end.

This is not the first importation of the serum. Some of it was brought by physicians to this city last September, and the Board of Health obtained a bottle of it, I believe. I should favor the application of the city's money to the manufacture of anti-toxine here, and the Board of Health is the proper department to undertake it.

In contrast to the moneymaking propensities of the physician who sells this life-saving remedy at $50 a dose, it is pleasant to relate that one of the men who to-day received a supply of the serum, got it for me, having learned that I was looking for some. He refused to receive any pay for it. As I am supplied, I shall, of course, return it to him, and retain a very pleasant remembrance of his act.

Aseptolin a New Remedy

BY THE NEW YORK TIMES | FEB. 8, 1896

DR. CYRUS EDSON announced yesterday, through the columns of The Medical Record and otherwise, the constituent parts of a new remedy for consumption.

It is claimed by Dr. Edson that the preparation which he has made will effect a radical cure of the disease under favorable conditions. In his communication to The Medical Record he enumerates 218 cases upon which the remedy has been tried, of which improvement has been noted in 212 and no improvement in 4 cases. Of the improved cases, 24 have been discharged as cured and 68 are believed to be in a fair way to recovery. In 91 of the remaining cases improvement has been noted, though not sufficient to warrant a definite opinion. In 32 cases the improvement was only temporary. There has been one death among the cases subject to the treatment.

Dr. Edson began his statement by referring to the fact that German chemists have found that carbolic acid is a normal secretion of the human body, which is enormously increased during disease. It occurred to him some time ago that this increase of carbolic acid in the excretions was an evidence of Nature's attempt to kill germs by the internal manufacture of a special substance poisonous to them.

Acting on this hint, Dr. Edson set himself to work to find a preparation of carbolic acid which would be borne by the human system in comparatively large doses, without giving rise to general poisoning effects.

Dr. Edson was encouraged in his selection of carbolic acid as the chief constituent of his remedy by the fact that many physicians have recently employed creosote as an active internal remedy for the cure of consumption. As creosote had been shown by the latest chemical researches to be in large part composed of carbolic acid, it occurred to Dr. Edson that whatever curative effects creosote had were due to the carbolic acid it contained.

The object which Dr. Edson then set before himself was to prepare carbolic acid in such a form that it might safely be injected into the tissues of the body by means of a hypodermic syringe. He calculated that with the large increase of carbolic acid in the body in cases of disease, a comparatively small additional quantity would be sufficient to reinforce it so as to enable the combined amount to stop the progress of consumption by killing off the germs of tuberculosis.

Finally, after a long series of experiments, Dr. Edson prepared a mixture containing 97.2 per cent, of water, 2.7 per cent, of carbolic acid, and .01 per cent, of a chemical compound of nearly equal parts of pilocarpine and carbolic acid. He gave this preparation the name of aseptolin.

Dr. Edson added the pilocarpine in order to increase the number of white blood corpuscles to stimulate the activity of the glands all over the body, and to stimulate expectoration and secretion.

Such, in brief, is the statement which was given out by Dr. Edson. The resulting liquid, as seen by a reporter for the New-York Times yesterday, is as transparent as water, of the consistency of thin syrup, and with the characteristic odor of carbolic acid.

Many physicians who were visited yesterday by the reporter expressed their satisfaction that Dr. Edson had discovered a cure for consumption, though they preferred to wait until a longer and more public trial of the new remedy could be had before placing themselves on record as favorable to it or the reverse.

It was only a little more than five years ago, as more than one of them reminded the reporter, since Kock, the greatest living bacteriologist, had given tuberculin to the world as a radical remedy, which had, after prolonged trials, turned to be a dismal failure in pulmonary consumption.

"Imagination," said one physician, "plays a great part in all new remedies for consumption. The patients are naturally so hopeful, owing to the character of the disease, that they will often gain in weight after a change in treatment, only to sink again as soon as their faith in the change disappears."

Dr. Biggs, the bacteriologist to the Health Board, was asked yesterday by the reporter if an examination of the new remedy came within the scope of his duties. He replied:

No. The Health Department has no concern with cures, as such. Our duty ends with aiding physicians to make a correct diagnosis where a bacteriological examination is necessary to settle definitely the presence or absence of certain pathogenic bacilli.

Thus we examine sputum to discover whether Koch's consumption bacilli are present or not. If they are present, the patient undoubtedly has tuberculosis; if not, the patient may have tuberculosis, but the fact is not proved by our examination.

"Leaving out Dr. Edson's new remedy, is there any radical cure for consumption?"asked the reporter.

"Yes," said Dr. Biggs;

pure air is a cure, and I have had many patients wholly and positively cured by this means. It does not matter much where you send a patient, in one sense, provided the air which he is to breathe is free from bacilli of all kinds. Of course, the general state of the patient's health makes one climate more desirable than another, but cures have been reported from the Adirondacks, from Colorado, from New-Mexico, from the Alps, and from Algiers.

Now, these places have absolutely nothing in common except their freedom from bacilli of all kinds. The same thing is true of a long sea voyage. It is curious that the health of patients improves more rapidly in the Adirondacks in Winter than in Summer, but that is because the snow is then on the ground, preventing the propagation of all the ordinary forms of bacilli.

Then, too, it is well to recollect that places which have become noted resorts for consumptives have, after their employment for a long term of years for this purpose, become regular death traps. That is because the bacilli of tuberculosis have been spread in all directions, and are inhaled by every inspiration made by the crowd of patients.

I heartily hope that Dr. Edson has succeeded in discovering a radical cure for consumption. It is my belief that most of the aggravated cases of consumption which we see in cities are complicated with other germ diseases which effect a lodgment after the consumption bacillus has made an entrance.

Another physician who did not care to have his name mentioned was inclined to believe that Dr. Edson's new remedy would turn out to be only palliative in its character.

"Dr. Declat, a French physician of note," he said,

tried hypodermic injections of carbolic acid twenty years ago for septicaemia. Now, the high temperature of consumption is septic in its character, due to the absorption of pus by the blood from the ulcer in the lung. The action of carbolic acid has hitherto been regarded as general in killing all kinds of bacilli.

If, then, Dr. Declat's method was allowed to fall into disuse by the accomplished physicians of Paris because it failed to stamp out the bacilli which cause septic inflammation, what hope is there that it will do any better in the special septic inflammation of tuberculosis?

I admit that the addition of pilocarpine is highly ingenious as tending to spread the carbolic solution through every part of the body, and also as giving it a chance to reach the cells when they are in a state of excessive activity due to the specific action of the pilocarpine.

But pilocarpine, which has been hailed in turn as a remedy for every disease, from rheumatism to cancer, has proved a comparative failure in all of these cases. If two drugs previously have been tried separately in cases where high temperatures have prevailed analogous to the septic or hectic fever of consumption without any permanent good results, is it likely that both of them combined will do what each has hitherto failed to accomplish?

The members of the medical profession in this city have known for several months past that Dr. Cyrus Edson had a preparation the composition of which he kept secret. Professional etiquette kept those physicians who take an interest in the treatment of phthisis from using Dr. Edson's remedy until he had made public its constituent parts and its method of preparation. As soon as the manufacturing chemists of the city have sufficient directions to enable them to manufacture it, some physicians are likely to give it a trial.

Modern Wound Treatment.

BY THE NEW YORK TIMES | JUNE 10, 1894

THE DAWN OF THE new treatment which was ultimately destined to revolutionize the whole subject of wound treatment, and to lead surgeons into paths of surgical enterprise which could never have been dreamed of in earlier times, was at hand. Sir (then Mr.) Joseph Lister was at work in his laboratory in Glasgow and in the wards of the Royal Infirmary at Glasgow. He had conceived the idea of the antiseptic treatment of wounds, and was engaged in elaborating out of it a system which ever since has borne his name. In brief, his method was based upon the assumption that the inflammatory changes occurring in a wound, associated with suppuration, were due to microbic infection. Here was a conviction which seemed to convey with it an infinity of problems, the solution of which might redound to the credit of surgery.

What a vast field for speculation and experiment is seemed to open out! The fact, however, having been established by incontrovertible scientific evidence that it was the presence of pathogenic germs in a wound which caused all those deplorable complications of blood poisoning, of which surgeons had so much to complain, the next step in the evolution of the system was comparatively an easy one. Naturally the only thing to be done was to insure the exclusion of all possible sources of infection. In order to arrive at this desirable condition of things, the most elaborate measures were deemed to be necessary. Evidently at the first a very serious view was taken of the wickedness of germs, and of their illimitable power to propagate evil.

The science of bacteriology could hardly then be said to be in existence, and all micro-organisms consequently were able to do very much as they pleased. But "their time came" when bacteriology blossomed into a science. The bacteriological laboratory is now the "Scotland Yard" of micro-organic life. There is so much known of the evil ways of germs that whenever an indefinable disease breaks out, or an

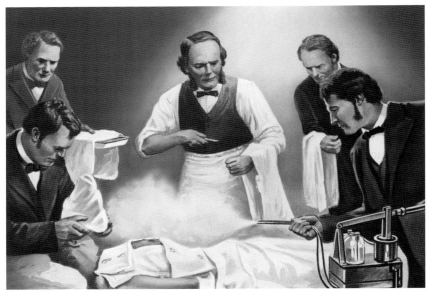

An illustration of Joseph Lister, center, directing use of carbolic acid spray in one of his earliest antiseptic surgical operations, circa 1865.

epidemic occurs, the first questions asked are: What and where is the germ? Then the bacteriologist, like the detective sent down from the central police office, proceeds to take up the case, and it is seldom now that he fails to drag the evildoer before the tribunal of science, and furnish proofs by which the micro-organism can be afterward identified.

The Roentgen Discovery

BY THE NEW YORK TIMES | FEB. 7, 1896

PRINCETON, N. J., FEB. 6. — Ever since the announcement of Prof. Roentgen's recent discovery of the remarkable effects of the so-called X-rays in photographic experiments, the members of the Faculty of Physics in the Princeton School of Science have been busily engaged with a series of experiments to test Prof. Roentgen's new discovery, and these experiments at Princeton have yielded some very interesting results.

Prof. W. F. Magie of the Department of Physics, under whose supervision most of the experiments have been conducted, expressed himself to-day as very highly gratified with the results obtained here. Among other things he exhibited a specimen photograph of his own hand, which had been photographed through a wooden board. Prof. Magie, in speaking of the practical application of Prof. Roentgen's discovery, said that, while its effectiveness had no doubt been greatly exaggerated, it will be of incalculable benefit in the medical profession. But here its usefulness will be largely confined to such things as locating foreign matter in the flesh, such as bullets. The similarity in point of opacity in the various internal organs of the body will render the X-rays of very little value in treating these organs. Prof. Magie said:

> The practical application of this great discovery may be summed up in one statement, viz., that, since different substances are opaque in different degrees to these rays, an assemblage of different bodies will make impressions of various degrees of intensity upon a photographic plate, and thus the presence of bodies concealed within others, about whose presence and exact position information is desired, can be deduced. It seems probable that the existence of blowholes or foreign substances in iron plates would thus be shown, or the exact position of a bullet in the arm or any part of the body through which this action can pass.

With respect to the apparatus which Prof. Magie has used in reaching his conclusions he had the following to say:

The apparatus that is used in Prof. Roentgen's remarkable investigations and by means of which most of them can be very easily repeated is of the simplest description. The Crooke tube is a tube of glass into which ordinarily, but not necessarily, are placed two wire terminals or electrodes, by means of which the current is introduced into the tube. The air is exhausted from the tube so that the vacuum in it is very good, but not complete. The discharge passes through this tube and appears around the negative electrode as a scarcely discernible bluish light, which sets up upon portions of the glass plate, on which it throws a brilliant phosphorescence. The new action of the so called X-rays of Prof. Roentgen apparently proceeds from the phosphorescent portion of the glass. The discharge here spoken of is that of the ordinary induction current of high electromotive force, produced by the ordinary inductricalor by the use of an electrical current and series of transformation.

The two ways of observing the new effect are by the aid of phosphorescent substances and by the photographic plate. If a sheet of paper coated with substances which can exhibit phosphorescence, is brought near a tube in which this discharge is going on, the tube being covered entirely with black paper, so that no light rays can escape from it, and the experiment being carried on in a dark room, it will appear luminous. The source of this luminosity is proved by Roentgen to be the wall of the tube, and the agent which excites proceeds in straight lines from this wall to the paper, so that objects interposed which to a greater or less extent check these rays, cast their shadows on the paper. The metals which intercept the rays most completely cast the darkest shadows, but light bodies appear opaque to these rays in some degree.

In order to obtain these shadows in permanent form an ordinary photographic plate may be substituted for the phosphorescent paper, and if the action be continued for a suitable time the plate may be developed, just as an ordinary photographic plate, when the shadow will he found permanently fixed on the plate. The X-rays pass readily through wood, and so the photographic plate contained in the ordinary plateholder, may be exposed to their action anywhere, not necessarily in a dark room.

The different permeability of various substances to these rays makes a contrast of shadows. Thus, for example, a coin in a purse will cast a darker shadow than the purse itself, and the bones in the hand a darker shadow than the flesh. In some respects these rays present peculiarities exhibited by no other known action in physics. They are apparently *not refracted, like light rays. If refracted at all, the refraction is very diffuse, and does not follow the ordinary law. On the other hand, they are not acted upon by magnets in the way in which the discharge within the Crooke tube is affected. Those who have had the best opportunity to observe them say positively that they cannot be of the nature of the discharge within the Crooke tube. The only theory which has thus far been advanced to explain them, is given very cautiously by Roentgen. He thinks it possible that there are longitudinal vibrations in the ether. Light is transmitted by vibrations transverse or across the line of progress, and, if Roentgen's theory is correct these new rays are, therefore, not of the nature of light. They are vibrations in the same medium as that which transmits light but are of a different nature.*

The older theory of light required such a longitudinal vibration, and the failure to discover one, was considered a serious defect in this theory. The new electro-magnetic theory of light, which has recently been so abundantly confirmed by the experiments of Hertz, do not require this longitudinal vibration. There is, perhaps, nothing in this later theory incompatible with the existence of longitudinal vibrations, but they do not form a necessary part of it. If they exist they are excited by an electrical disturbance different in kind from that which sets up light rays. Lord Kelvin pointed out, some years ago, as has been shown by Mr. Bottomly, that a view of the structure of ether might be taken by which such waves (which we may call waves of electrical condensation and rarefication) may exist. Too little is known as yet of this new action to progress with any decision upon the question of its origin.

Prof. Magie will continue his experiments with a view to confirming certain theories of his own in respect to the new discovery which he is not yet ready to announce.

WITHOUT THE CROOKE TUBE.
Results of Experiments by W. D. Crumbie with the Roentgen Rays.

The latest experiment with Roentgen rays, made by W. D. Crumbie, tends to show that images can be formed of concealed metals without the intervention of a Crooke tube.

Mr. Crumbie first tried two experiments with dry negative plates, enclosed in their usual cover when not intended for an exposure, and having coins slipped in between the cover and the plate. He then placed a Crooke tube in front of the case containing the negative.

The first exposure was for thirty minutes and proved a complete failure. A change was then made in the apparatus, a brass plate being attached to the negative wire which had previously been joined to the cathode of the Crooke tube, while the positive wire leading to the anode remained as before. In this case an indistinct image of one of the coins was found on the dry plate after an exposure of thirty minutes.

In the third experiment, the Crooke tube was omitted and two brass plates were attached, one to each wire. The case containing the coins and the negative plate were placed between these plates and the current allowed to run for thirty minutes. At the end of that length of time the outlines of the two coins contained in the case were plainly visible in the developed negatives. The edges were as clearly marked as If they had been printed.

Mr. Crumbie's deduction from these experiments is that the Roentgen photographs are due to action in the magnetic field, and not to the X-rays from the Crooke tube.

A Cure for Snakebite.

FROM THE PALL MALL GAZETTE | MARCH 27, 1898

DR. CALMETTE, WHO WAS, some years ago, one of the most brilliant pupils of Pasteur, and is the brother of M. Gaston Calmette, the well-known writer on the Figaro, is credited with having made an important medical discovery, namely, that of a perfectly efficacious antidote for snakebite. This consists of a 1 per cent solution of chloride of gold, ten drops of which injected into a guinea pig, pigeon, or rabbit immediately suffices to destroy the toxic nature of a drop of the snake venom. Five to ten cubic centimeters of the solution are sufficient to counteract the poison of a bite which is fatal to a dog, a monkey, and probably to a man. The dose has no ill effects. It causes no pain, and by increasing it, absolute immunity from the poison is obtained. The sole condition to be fulfilled is that the solution should be reliable, sterilized, and kept in a dark vial to preserve it from the influence of sunlight. It is injected with an ordinary hypodermic syringe.

Dr. Calmette, who is Director of the Bacterioiogical Institute at Saigon, has been engaged for some time past in the study of antidotes for various microbic diseases, notably cholera and the pest.

The Triumphs of Surgery

BY THE NEW YORK TIMES | OCT. 10, 1897

DR. LEWIS A. SAYRE, the oldest of the famous surgeons of the United States, is enjoying life at the age of seventy-eight. He has been for more than half a century a participator in and observer of those surgical operations which have made the American scalpel renowned for skill and audacity.

> When I was a student under Dr. Green in 1839," said Dr. Sayre, "a hurry call came for him. I went down to the docks and found the cabin boy lying senseless on the deck of a vessel then just on the point of sailing. The lad had fallen from the masthead, breaking his thigh on the yardarm and striking his head against the edge of the poop. The boy's left frontal bone was stove in and (his face covered) with blood. Novice though I was, I saw that instant action was needed. Seizing an oyster knife, I pried up, as best I could, the broken and depressed edges of the fracture, and had the boy taken to the Old New York Hospital in Broadway, opposite Pearl Street.

HIS FIRST KNOWLEDGE OF TREPHINING.

> Dr. Gurdon Buck speedily trephined the boy's skull. No sooner had he picked up the broken bone and relieved the pressure on the brain than the cabin boy began to speak in English, asking: 'What are you doing there?'
>
> We all know, now, that the third convolution of the left side of the brain is the seat of the faculty of speech, but in 1839 the functions of the brain were not localized. So I marveled at this strange result. Presently hernia cerebri, a swelling out of the brain through the wound, set in, and this caused the skillful surgeon more trouble, to overcome which Dr. Buck cut from a sheet of thin lead a circular piece large enough to cover the wound, and, gently forcing the protruding brain back into its place, bandaged the lead over the gaping aperture in the skull.
>
> Another complication set in. Pus formed; for pus always formed in wounds in those days long antedating antisepsis, and Dr. Buck, to release the pus without removing the lead, cut in the centre of the latter

a slit, into which a sixpence might have been inserted edgewise, and this drained the pus. Nature helped, too, and the boy made a fine recovery, and was kept in the hospital for some time thereafter as an illustration of what skillful surgery could do in those days.

A SURGEON'S TOO CLEAR EXPLANATION.

The College of Physicians and Surgeons where I was attending lectures was at 65 Crosby Street, near Spring. Dr. Watts was the lecturer on anatomy, and I said something to him one day about the talks which accompanied the operations at the New York Hospital not being explicit and full enough to give the students a clear idea of what was going on in the operating table. Dr. Watts told Dr. Post about what I had said, and the next time he operated he went into an elaborate exposition of flaps and circular flaps, the application of the tourniquet in amputations, the stoppage of hemorrhage by hot iron, round ligatures and flat ligatures, and the various kinds of amputations.

The operating table then, as now, was in the centre of an amphitheatre, upon whose sides rose tiers of seats. It happened that on this particular day I knew the subject who was going to be operated on after Dr. Post's lucid explanations were finished, for, as in the cabin boy's case, I had been the means of bringing him in to the hospital. So I could not help noticing that the subject, as he lay on the operating table, waiting in full possession of all his faculties for the knife to cut into his leg, was listening quite as intently as I myself to the big words that poured from Dr. Post's lips, and glanced now and then from the bright catlings (operating knives) to the tourniquet, which had in the meantime been put on his leg by Dr. Alexander H. Stevens, the consulting surgeon. There were no such things as anaesthetics in those days, and the big lout of a fellow was growing whiter and more nervous every minute of Dr. Post's eloquence. He first looked at me, then, at his legs, and then at the door, his eyes fairly popping from his head.

All of a sudden, to my horror, as Dr. Post advanced, catling in hand, the fellow bounded from the operating table, crying, 'Get me me breeches, be gob; I'll die with my leg on!' and before any body quite realized what was going on he was half way to the door.

"I ran after him as hard as I could, and after me came Dr. Dixon, editor of The Scalpel. 'Go back there, go back there, this instant,' he called out to our subject; 'you shan't disappoint all those students!' and I, too, threatened him with Dr. Green's displeasure and begged him to return; but it was of no use. The fellow had his breeches on by this time, and was half way out of the door. Being an Irishman, he saw something of the humor of the situation himself; so, as he went out, he turned and called back to the students, 'I'm sorry to disapp'int ye, gintlemen, but by God's help I'll die with me leg on,' and with that he was gone.

A CASE FOR THE YOUNG SURGEON.

Here was a pretty mess, indeed, all over Dr. Post's explicit statement of what he was going to do. Kearney Rodgers talked a good deal, Cheeseman scarcely talked at all, but Post had, indeed, talked to good purpose. Even the subject understood him.

The sufferer — I can now apply that term to him designedly — was the foreman of a fire company who had come a cropper as his engine was dashing, lickety-split, from the engine house in Watts Street, near Canal, down Greenwich Street. The leg got worse and worse, and by and by Dr. Green was sent for to see him, and I made the call with him. We found the man suffering intensely in a dive in Watts Street, near Canal, stretched out on an old horse-hair sofa.

It did not take Dr. Green long to come to the conclusion that the knee had been neglected so long that nothing but amputation would now relieve him.

WILLARD PARKER'S TIMELY LECTURE.

Now, having refused to submit his leg to the catling, the unfortunate foreman was on my hands again, and I can't say that I expected to put him on his feet. I can't do anything more for him, sonny,' Dr. Green said to me. 'You must do the best you can.' I was wondering just what I could do with the tremendous swelling of the poor fellow's knee, when Dr. Willard Parker began his lecture that morning.

To my surprise and gratification, Dr. Parker talked to us about the 'tactus eruditus,' the touch of experience, the right method of applying it, and its usefulness in detecting pus. I resolved to try the 'tactus eruditus' on my patient in Watts Street.

When we went down to the New York Hospital that day Dr. Buck, who was about to operate, applied the 'tactus eruditus' and showed us how he determined where pus had formed, and then opened the swelling above and below and put a drainage tube through it. The immediate relief experienced by the patient made a deep impression on me.

"On leaving the hospital I went around to my Watts Street patient. I tried the 'tactus eruditus' on the foreman's knee, as Dr. Parker had instructed, and then I set about opening the swelling, as I had seen Dr. Buck do. I made a longitudinal slash, the pus spurted out over my shoulder, and the patient was evidently much relieved. I scraped lint, bound up the wound as best I could, having provided, as I thought, for its drainage, and then went home and told Dr. Green what I had done.

SURGICAL PRECEDENTS VIOLATED.

My preceptor swore a blue streak. 'My God, Kentuck, he said, 'you have opened the joint, something surgery abhors, a thing no surgeon ever did in the world! Kentuck, go butt your head against a stone wall, and put shavings where your brains ought to be!' He often called me Kentuck, as I had been brought up by an uncle in Kentucky. You may depend upon it I felt blue enough by this time, for I had not aspired to be a pioneer in surgery.

I wandered dejectedly around to Watts Street, expecting to find my man in a woeful plight.

Lo and behold, when I reached him he was better, much better, he said. I scraped more lint and dressed the wound, gave him some oysters, and left him feeling comfortable.

Dr. Willard Parker's next lecture at the 'P. and S.' was on 'Chronic Abscesses' and he laid down the law that under no circumstances must a surgeon ever cut open a swollen joint. This confirmation, so speedily, of what Dr. Green had said about my opening the fireman's kneejoint convinced me that I was little short of a murderer, and I hurried away to Watts Street in fear and trembling. I found my patient lying on a musty old horse-hair sofa, with his leg stretched out on a chair. He was in pain and glad to see me, and I went about dressing his wound with a lighter heart. The lint had caked and hardened in the wound so tight that the pus had not been able to escape. I soaked it with hot water until the lint came loose, and once more, the pus spurted out and the pain was relieved.

ACCIDENT THAT LED TO A DISCOVERY.

I had been buying lint at the drug store at the corner of Varick and Canal Streets. When I looked about me, realizing that on this particular day I had neither lint nor money to purchase it, my eyes fell on the tow stuffing sticking out of the old horse-hair sofa. I took some of that tow and used it instead of lint in dressing the fireman's knee.

Next day, when I came to dress the wound again, I had plenty of lint with me. I found the wound open and free from pus, absolutely different from what it had been when dressed with lint. I could only conclude that the tow had caused the difference, siphoning the wound out by capillary attraction. I reasoned from this that tow dipped in Peruvian balsam would not only disinfect a wound, owing to the creosote in the balsam, but would keep it free from pus. And this was the foundation of one of the most satisfactory successes I have ever had in surgery. Later on my experience convinced me of the value of hemp, as an improvement on tow, and that was the means of introducing into the army the use of tarred hemp, or oakum, as a dressing for wounds, by which many thousand lives were saved.

My fireman got well, and for twenty years sold apples from a stand at the corner of Broadway and Prince Street.

THE TWO GREATEST DISCOVERIES.

"Doctor," I asked, "what are the greatest benefits surgery has conferred on mankind?"

"Antiseptics and anaesthetics," was Dr. Sayre's prompt reply.

Had we understood antisepsis in the times of the war as we understand it now, the lives of a large percentage of the wounded who died from their wounds could have been saved. In all surgical operations before Lister's discoveries, about thirty years ago, when antisepsis was practically introduced into surgery, the operator's instruments were prepared for his work by dipping into water and then rubbing dry on a towel, as clean as possible. Every precaution, indeed, was taken against infection except those antiseptic precautions which are now considered essential. Of course, under those conditions pus formed invariably in wounds. Nowadays, thanks to antiseptics, pus is unknown. Two years ago, I recall, Dr. Stephen Smith wanted to lecture on pus and show the students at Bellevue the actual difference between laudable and illaudable pus, and he searched the hospital high and low, but couldn't find a particle of pus in the whole place. The results of surgery have indeed become almost mathematical.

MOST BENEFICENT OPERATIONS.

Dr. Sayre was asked what are the most important and beneficent surgical operations ever performed in the United States. Without a moment's hesitation he answered:

First of all, the operation of ovariotomy, done by Dr. McDowell of Kentucky, in a rustic community, unaided by assistants, trained nurses, or surgical equipments, in the year 1810 or 1812. A Mrs. Crawford went to Dr. McDowell one day in the little town of Danville, Ky., then nothing but a hamlet, and asked his advice. He diagnosed a tumor, in such a position that nothing short of an operation then unheard of, undreamed of, I may say, could be of service to her.

Born and bred in the country, Dr. McDowell had been accustomed to seeing heifers spayed to prevent maternity. He thought it over and could see no reason why a similar operation should not prove successful in a human being. He then explained the situation frankly to Mrs. Crawford and her family, and she, brave woman that she was, told the Doctor to go ahead and do the best he could for her. The operation was entirely and absolutely successful, and Mrs. Crawford lived for many years. Dr. Gaillard Thomas has said that this operation has added 40,000 years to human life.

FIRST HIPJOINT EXSECTION.

The first hipjoint ever exsected successfully in this country was in 1854. I had long wanted to perform the operation, but the doctors wouldn't come to see it. They ridiculed the exsection of a hipjoint as they had ridiculed the cutting out of an ovarian tumor. I explained, to the father of my patient — her name was Ellen Guyon, and she is now living — just what I proposed to do, and he gave his consent. He was an engineer in the Morgan Iron Works. I performed the operation, which was entirely successful, and in the thirty-three years that have since elapsed I have performed it seventy-four times.

THE TEST FOR LAPAROTOMY.

Dr. Senn of Milwaukee, now of Chicago, I consider one of our greatest surgeons. At a recent meeting of the American Medical Association, in Cincinnati, Dr. Senn brought in a dog, and, pulling out a pistol, shot the animal point blank through the abdomen. He then inflated the dog's intestines with hydrogen gas, through the rectum, and, holding a match in front of its lips ignited the gas, showing that the animal had not been perforated by the bullet and that the operation of laparotomy was not necessary.

Dr. Senn then shot another dog in the abdomen from another direction, and gave it the hydrogen gas. This time a lighted match placed at creature's lips showed that no flame resulted. The intestines were shown to be perforated. Instantly performing laparotomy on both dogs, Dr. Senn demonstrated that his deductions had been correct and that the test could be used by the profession throughout the country as a test of whether laparotomy ought to be performed when men and women are shot through the abdomen. This operation of laparotomy for gunshot wounds was first performed by Dr. William T. Bull, at the Chambers Street Hospital in New York, a comparatively few years ago as Dr. Bull is a young man now. He made a great success of it.

NO RESTRICTIONS TO SURGICAL SKILL.

"Dr. Sayre, what are the human ailments that have most persistently refused to yield to human skill?"

Tuberculosis, I should say, was the first. There are so-called cures, just as there are so-called cures of alcoholism.

There are, however, no organs, no parts of the human frame to which the surgeon's knife is not now applied on proper occasions. Heart, brain, lungs, spleen, liver and kidneys are cut, healed, and treated as necessity demands. No man may say, now that the usefulness of the X-rays has been demonstrated in surgery, what limitations of restrictions are to be placed on human skill and daring.

CHAPTER 2

Microbes, the Mind and Research: 1900–1929

The turn of the twentieth century brought with it increasing excitement in medical advances. World War I (1914–1918), with its mass movement of troops and the housing of large numbers of soldiers, provided a fertile environment for an increase in disease, just as wars have throughout history. Yet a new vaccine for typhus lowered the death count while other vaccines tackled malaria and scarlet fever. The ability to view microbes with the human eye sharpened the focus of medical research. The cause of rickets was identified as a lack of Vitamin D, a previously unknown vitamin. New treatments promised to help with diabetes and pneumonia while improvements in psychiatry and the study of the heart also occurred.

The Phipps Psychiatric Clinic.

BY THE NEW YORK TIMES | JUNE 25, 1908

DR. ADOLPH MEYER, whose appointment as Director of the projected Phipps Clinic of Psychiatry at Johns Hopkins was this week made known, is of opinion that its work will "open up boundless opportunities for the treatment of curable mental disorders." Dr. William Hanna Thomson, writing in Everybody's Magazine for July on the relation of the nervous system to the blood, laments that no institution of the kind is yet in actual operation. Dr. Thomson declares that recent discoveries about nervous affections have put medicine in the position of "Columbus when he first landed on a West Indian Isle," an island that "belonged to a great new world."

These discoveries refer to the fact that, in its normal state, the body is its own physician and pharmacist, daily manufacturing powerful drugs which repel external invasions and suppress internal disturbances. For specific purposes, as of digestion, it makes its own poisons and pours into the blood their antidotes, as well as special antidotes for the poisons brought in by bacteria. The body diagnoses, prescribes, and compounds for itself in a precise scheme of remedy and prevention. When disturbed in this function by extraordinary inroads of microbic disease, or by excesses of eating or drinking, the blood stream becomes vitiated, and the working parts of the brain and other organs are clogged. This, in fine, is the new doctrine of functional nervous diseases of the familiar type of hysteria, epilepsy, neurasthenia, and dyspepsia.

The neurologist, it seems, has thus invaded the field of physiological chemistry. Dr. Thomson finds that the sympathetic nervous ganglia, ranged along the spine, lying back of the important organs, and irradiating in many thousands of knots through every tissue, control the body's drug-producing activities. If this be true, the clinic at Johns Hopkins will have its province in clearing up questions, now certainly obscure, of how this nervous control is exercised and how it is lost in types of disease.

Microbes Caught in Action.

SPECIAL CABLE TO THE NEW YORK TIMES | OCT. 31, 1909

PARIS, OCT. 30. — Moving pictures of the smallest micro-organisms discernable through the most perfect of magnifying instruments have been made by Jean Comandon, a young French scientist. His work was duly reported to the Academy of Sciences at its last session, causing more open wonderment than is usually expressed by that body of cool-blooded savants.

The baccilli first represented were one-thousandth of a milimeter in length. They are known as tripanozomes, and inhabit the blood of mice who have been inoculated with the sleeping sickness. Thirty-two cinematographs per second were taken by Comandon of these almost infinitely little creatures and images were projected upon the screen on a scale of 20,000 diameters. One drop of the blood of a mouse placed between two plates of glass sufficed to furnish endless variations of animate motion. A flea pictured on the same proportion would look as big as a six-story house. But other baccilli were also represented in the same manner, including several types found in the blood of human beings.

Prof. Dastre, member of the Academy of Sciences, said:

> The consequences of Comandon's discovery are incalculable. All the activities of microbes, including the Brownian movements, which are so little understood, can now be studied with a precision hitherto inconceivable. Physiological questions of the greatest importance, impossible of elucidation in the past, can probably be solved by this new method.

Lister's War on Pain and Death

REVIEW | BY THE NEW YORK TIMES | FEB. 18, 1912

The man who died last week made it easier for other men to live.

SURGICALLY SPEAKING, WE live in the Listerian age. This simple statement of fact is accepted without quibble by every physician and surgeon in the world; but a definition of it is necessary for the layman. It means, then, that we live in an age when 99 per cent of those who have been obliged to undergo major operations — that is, operations involving the amputation of a limb, the opening of the abdominal or thoracic cavities, or something equally serious — recover. Prior to the Listerian age the death rate was one in three following such operations. Truly, a marvelous revolution in surgical procedure is here revealed. Listerism saves more lives every year than Napoleon destroyed in all his wars.

There is one thing about Listerism even more astonishing: Lord Lister himself, the founder of Listerism, the father of antiseptic surgery, lived in the Listerian age. He died last week, but he had lived to see criticism of his theories, his methods, and his triumphs die. He died secure in the knowledge that the world of science had recognized in him one of the greatest benefactors of mankind. No long drawn out century of pain intervened before the general adoption of antiseptic and aseptic surgery.

Almost on the eve of Lord Lister's death Dr. C. W. Saleeby, a well-known writer of books on medical topics and one who sat at the feet of Lister, published a work entitled "Surgery and Society, A Tribute to Listerism." In it he has traced the history of pre-Listerian surgery; the work of Pasteur, which made Lister's discoveries possible; the theories and methods of Lister, and discusses also many other interesting things relating to the surgical practice of to-day.

In Dr. Saleeby's opinion, Listerism has averted as much pain as anaesthesia because inflammation is painful. The thing that Lister did, therefore, was to abolish inflammation, sepsis, or blood poisoning, following operations. Two things have robbed surgery of its terrors — anaesthesia and the antiseptic methods of operating. Surgical anaesthesia was first employed by Morton in Boston in 1847. Lister first used carbolic acid as an antiseptic in 1868.

Prior to the discovery of these two humanitarian measures surgery was a living horror, especially on the battlefield. Midnight amputations by the dim light of lanterns in the open beneath a wintry sky followed each other by the score. The most primitive dressings were used, and the best that could be promised was to arrest the flow of blood. Of the heroic men who submitted to this well-meant butchery fully 90 per cent died.

As the author justly says, although Louis Pasteur was a chemist and bacteriologist and not a physician or surgeon, "he is the father of all physicians and surgeons worthy of the name to-day." He evolved the microbic theory of disease. Many of the most malignant ailments, he declared, are caused by germs. We know them now by various names — bacilli, cocci, spirilla, and so on. Lister, professor of surgery in Glasgow University, eagerly embraced this theory. It seemed to him also that germs were responsible for the putrefactive changes resulting in post-operative inflammation, sepsis, and death. He even thought that the air itself must be impregnated with these malignant microbes. They must be combated, but how was it to be done?

Lister had great faith in carbolic acid as the agent most likely to destroy microbes. He used it in strong solutions and very freely. The author speculates on the ravages this powerful drug must have made on the hands of the operators. After the operative surface had been plentifully sprinkled with the acid, Lister warned his assistants that they must imagine everything as smeared with green paint. This was to impress upon them the necessity for keeping their hands and every other possible source of contamination away from the neighborhood of the operative surface and the surgical wound. It magnified the idea of the ubiquity of the microbes.

Not satisfied with these precautions, the great surgeon operated while enveloped in a cloud of carbolic acid spray which was constantly played upon operator, patient, and operating table alike. The day this procedure was carried out marked an epoch in the history of surgery. Wonderful results were achieved, and improvements in technique and the substitution of other drugs for carbolic acid have continued ever since. Nor has perfection yet been attained.

In the following year Lister was called to the University of Edinburgh, then the light of the medical and surgical world.

Later he demonstrated his methods at King's College, London. Like many other pioneers of science, he was subjected to bitter criticism. There were disciples, however, among enlightened nations, such as France and Denmark, to promulgate his doctrines. And so his fame and teachings spread; his star shone brightest at the hour of his death and its glory can never fade.

Dr. Saleeby finds much to criticise in the attitude of many British subjects toward the science of to-day, and in particular he condemns the anti-vivisectionists of England. His work is a timely and needed tribute to Listerism, and can be read with profit by both physicians and laymen.

—

SURGERY AND SOCIETY: A Tribute to Listerism.
By C. W. Saleeby, M. D., R. F. S. E.
Moffat, Yard & Co. $2.50.

New Discoveries May Eliminate Quinine for Malaria

BY THE NEW YORK TIMES | JULY 13, 1913

SCIENTISTS HAVE DEFINITELY established the fact that malaria has frequently been a potent factor in changing the history of the world. This devastating scourge has been held responsible in some quarters for the downfall of at least one great nation. Towns and villages have disappeared in the face of its ravages, while cultivated lands have become barren wastes, shunned by all men, because they have become the breeding places of the poisonous mosquitoes which spread this disease.

In our own time, as well as in the remote ages of antiquity, malaria has proved the greatest stumbling block in the march of human progress. Thanks to modern sanitation, this stumbling block can now be removed by patient effort. The history of the Panama Canal Zone proves that long before it was discovered that a species of mosquito deposited the malarial protozoa in the blood it had been learned that quinine was a specific for malaria itself.

Apparently content with this knowledge, science neglected the study of malaria to a great extent and it was not until a few years ago that the laboratory workers started in to elucidate the mystery of the toxic activity in the blood which produced, with unfailing sequence, the chill, the fever, and the sweating, the three characteristic symptoms of malaria. The often repeated cycle of these classic symptoms resulted in a prostration due to anaemia, which, in turn, depended upon the destruction of large quantities of blood cells of different varieties. So in vast areas in different parts of the world we find large percentages of the inhabitants suffering from what may be called locally malaria, chills and fever, or fever and ague.

Aided by a grant from the Rockefeller Institute for Medical Research, Dr. Wade H. Brown has been carrying on a series of experiments for the last two years or more in the Pharmacological

Laboratory of the University of Wisconsin, Madison, Wis., and the Pathological Laboratory of the University of North Carolina, Chapel Hill, N. C., in the endeavor to discover what part the malarial pigment, hematin, plays as a factor in the production of the malarial paroxysm. These experiments have been attended with the most brilliant results and warrant the assumption that a more effective and less harmful agent than quinine may be discovered for the treatment of malaria. If such an agent is found, it will be the result of exact scientific procedure and not the whim of chance, as was the case when it was discovered that quinine would conquer the disease.

WHAT IS HEMATIN?

What, then, is hematin? It is "a brownish blood-pigment," according to the dictionaries, "the acid radicle which unites with globin to form hemoglobin." In other words, it is a constituent of the solid part of the blood — a part of the blood corpuscles — and it is set free when the hemoglobin of the red blood corpuscles is decomposed. When thus set free by decomposition, hematin acts as a poison.

Before Dr. Brown began his experiments it had been demonstrated that the blood became possessed of toxic properties coincident with the segmentation of the malarial parasite (plasmodium malariae) in the blood. In other words, these toxic properties manifested themselves at the exact time of the birth of a new generation of malarial parasites in the blood. In a contribution to The Journal of Experimental Medicine in 1911 Dr. Brown showed that the pigment elaborated from the hemoglobin of the red blood corpuscle and liberated into the circulation of the host at the time of segmentation of the parasite was undoubtedly hematin. He noted also that a rabbit that had received an intravenous injection of alkaline hematin developed a shaking chill very like that of malaria.

It occurred to him immediately that hematin might be one of the hypothetical toxins operative in malaria. He thereupon made a series of ninety observations with eighteen rabbits to discover the effects of the intravenous injection of alkaline hematin. The details of this experimentation were given in a contribution to The Journal of Experimental Medicine, which appeared in June, 1912. These are the conclusions he had reached at that time:

1. Alkaline hematin in doses commensurate with the amounts of hematin liberated in the human circulation by the segmentation of the malarial parasite produces, when injected intravenously into the rabbit, a paroxysm which is characterized by a short prodromal stage, a stage of chill and rising temperature, and a hot stage. In their details the phases of this paroxysm are practically identical with the corresponding ones in the paroxysm of human malaria.

2. The phenomena in human beings infected with malaria (are, at least in part, directly referable to the toxic action of this malarial pigment).

Not content to let the matter rest at this stage of the investigation, Dr. Brown carried on still other experiments in the laboratory, the results of which are announced in the current issue of The Journal of Experimental Medicine under the heading "Malarial Pigment (Hematin) as an Active Factor of the Blood Pigment of Malaria." This goes more particularly into the action of the liberated hematin on the different varieties of corpuscles, or cells, that are found in the blood. This is the investigator's summary of the latest series of experiments:

1. Intravenous injections of alkaline hematin in the rabbit produce an anaemia the severity of which is proportional to the amount of hematin injected and the susceptibility of the animal.

2. Hemoglobinemia (the presence of free hemoglobin in the blood plasma) is an occasional consequence of hematin poisoning.

3. The leucocytes in hematin intoxication are usually increased in number and are always characterized by a high percentage of large mononuclear cells and by pigmented phagocytes.

4. The platelets are markedly decreased by alkaline hematin, and ultimately a prolongation of the bleeding time results.

5. The anaemia, the hemoglobinemia, the high percentage of large mononuclear leucocytes, the destruction of platelets, and the tendency to hemorrhage in malaria are all influenced by the malaria pigment, hematin.

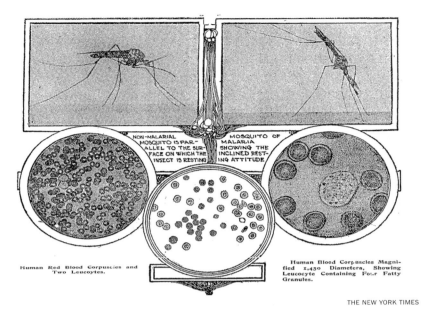

Depictions of mosquitos and magnifications of human blood corpuscles. The magnification at center shows the effects of malarial poison on human blood corpuscles.

The technical language of the laboratory, as revealed in this summary, brings forcibly to the attention of the layman the fact that there are more elements in the blood than the majority of us were permitted to know from our casual acquaintance with physiology in high school days.

Dr. Brown calls attention to the fact in his 1912 article that in spite of the enormous amount of investigation that has centred about the malarial parasite and its relation to malarial fevers, there has come no clear exposition of the mode of production of the various phenomena of the malarial paroxysm. It is true, however, as he states, that these phenomena have been ascribed to the presence in the circulation of some toxic substance or substances, elaborated by the malarial parasite.

It is probable that the very failure to penetrate the secret of the toxic action of the malaria parasite on the blood, previous to Dr. Brown's brilliant laboratory work, is responsible in no small degree for the great strides that have been made in the prevention of malaria by the employment of the methods devised by the sanitarian. Great areas have been made safely habitable by these measures, and the tasks of civilized man, such as the construction of the Madeira River Railroad in South America and the Panama Canal, can be carried on without the check and hindrance that were the dread of former times.

POSSIBLE DEVELOPMENT.

It is likely, however, in view of the discoveries of Dr. Brown, that renewed efforts will be made to attack the problem in the laboratory. It is easily within the bounds of probability that within a decade some bio-chemical product will be evolved, an antitoxin in the form of a vaccine or a serum, that will effectually dispose of the toxins of malaria. Indeed, a vaccine may be produced which will protect humanity from the dreaded onslaught of the malaria-carrying mosquito quite as effectively as vaccination against smallpox.

Divested of technical language, Dr. Brown's procedure was to prepare solutions of certain strengths of hematin derived from three sources, rabbit blood, dog blood, and ox blood. The rabbits used received doses by injection, as nearly comparable as possible to the doses of hematin liberated into the human circulation at the time of segmentation of a generation of parasites. Previous to these injections a preliminary series of experiments had been carried on to determine, as nearly as possible, the normal temperature of rabbits. This differs widely in different rabbits, but the normal temperature of each animal, with its natural fluctuations, was fixed as accurately as possible.

In estimating the temperature effects of hematin in all instances at least three facts had to be taken into consideration: The nature of the effect, the degree of the effect, and the duration of the effect, remembering always that the classical division of the malarial paroxysm is into a cold stage, a hot stage, and a stage of sweating.

"Without exception," says Dr. Brown, "every dose of hematin administered has elicited a definite temperature response. With but three exceptions this response has been characterized by a sharp rise in temperature reaching the fastigium (acme) in about an hour and a quarter."

After further details the investigator says that the extent of the temperature elevation is, within certain limits, proportional to the amount of hematin injected.

"The temperature effect," he observes, "being very slight with small doses, increases with the dose until we begin to obtain signs of an overintoxication, when the elevation may be much less than with smaller doses, the optimum dose usually being between 10 and 15 milligrams per kilo of body weight."

Where the reactions from the hematin were well marked the temperature usually returned to the normal range in the course of three to five hours.

"Apart from the elevation of temperature in the experimental animal," the investigator continues, "the paroxysm of hematin intoxication presents other features which are of equal importance and show a strong resemblance to corresponding phenomena of the malarial paroxysm. For the first fifteen or twenty minutes following the injection of hematin the rabbit usually manifests a slight degree of restlessness, then crouches in a corner of the cage. In the second stage of the paroxysm the vessels of the ears contract, giving to the ears a pale and cyanotic hue, while at the same time the ears become decidedly cold. During this stage the animal's ears usually lie on its back, and the hair tends to become erect, presenting the picture of an animal that is cold. Meanwhile the rabbit shows convulsive tremors or shivering, but rarely any continued or pronounced shaking."

The stage of chill lasts from forty-five minutes to an hour, when the superficial vessels abruptly dilate and the animal's ears become flushed and hot. It soon became apparent that repeated injections of a given dose of hematin in the same animal did not give uniform results. These results were of a nature to suggest that the animal acquired a certain degree of tolerance which, in turn, might be broken when the intoxication was pushed sufficiently. That this was the fact was determined by subsequent experimentation.

As a result of the ninety observations recorded in last year's article, Dr. Brown prepared this summary:

The paroxysm of hematin intoxication in the rabbit undoubtedly presents many features of striking similarity to the paroxysm of human malaria; still one must hesitate to apply such results unreservedly in an attempt to identify the causative agent of the malarial paroxysm. When, in addition to the character of the paroxism, we consider the sequence events in the two instances, the analogy becomes so close that it seems impossible to regard the matter as a mere coincidence! The injection of hematin, especially in fractional doses, is in a measure comparable to the liberation of hematin into the human circulation by the malarial parasite. In these experiments both solution and finely divided suspensions of hematin have been found equally effective in eliciting the phenomena of the paroxysm, and while it seems possible that a portion of the malarial pigment might be dissolved in the alkaline human serum, such an assumption is probably not essential.

It might be objected that the toxic action of foreign hematin thus injected into the circulation would probably be greater than that of hematin derived from an animal's own blood, but, so far as I have been able to determine, this objection does not seem valid, as rabbit hematin, dog hematin, and ox hematin produce in the rabbit effects that are alike in both character and degree.

The dose of hematin remains as the one factor to which it is possible to attach some degree of uncertainty, but even here the author feels that the range of experimental conditions has been kept within the bounds of legitimate analogy with conditions existing in the human subject of malarial infection.

Finally, the most conservative estimate of the value of such experiments points strongly to the fact that we have at least a potentially toxic substance in the pigment hematin as liberated by the malarial parasite into the circulation of the human host.

There is also abundant evidence to show that the action of hematin is not confined to the paroxysmal phenomena of malaria, but that other features of the disease may find their explanation in the action of this pigment. For the present, however, it seems advisable to confine the discussion to this one phase of the question.

In his further study of the effects of hematin upon the blood Dr. Brown gives further evidence of the role that it plays in malaria, and gives the details of a series of experiments, which he concludes with this discussion of the subject:

> Comparing the various phases of the effect of alkaline hematin upon the blood of the rabbit with the blood in malaria fevers, it cannot be claimed that there is an absolute identity, and yet there are no very great differences. The characteristic anemia of malaria has been ascribed to several accessory causes apart from the destruction of the red cells by the parasite developing within them. Prominent among these accessory pauses has been the theory of a circulating toxin, destructive to the red cells.
>
> Hematin fulfills the essential conditions for such a circulating toxin, and it is only remarkable that this pigment should cause so pronounced an anemia as it has been found capable of producing. In this connection, it does not seem amiss again to call attention to the fact that the hemoglobin converted to hematin by the malarial parasite is not readily available for the regeneration of red cells, and the blood in this manner is rapidly depleted of hemoglobin iron. This condition undoubtedly contributes to the perpetuation of the malaria anemia.
>
> Concerning the influence of hematin upon the leucocytes of malaria, one can speak with less assurance. In the first place, the possible normal variations of these cells in the rabbit are very great. Added to this is the influence of alkaline salt solution, which is difficult to estimate, and finally the difficulty of adjusting the dose of hematin so as to produce desired degrees of intoxication. Therefore only broad generalizations seem to be permissible.
>
> The leucocytosis of hematin poisoning is in sharp contrast to the leucopenia of the milder forms of malaria, but it coincides with the leucocytosis of the pernicious forms. The increase in the large mononuclear leucocytes, which is so characteristic of malarial blood, is also a prominent feature of the blood hematin intoxication.
>
> Although the percentage of these cells is probably not as high as in malaria, this would hardly be expected as there are certainly other causes that contribute to the increase in large mononuclear leucocytes. Finally, the general cycle of changes produced by an injection of hematin is, at least qualitatively, analogous to changes occurring in the blood with the paroxysm of malaria. Altogether, it would seem that hematin must play some part in the determination of the leucocyte picture of malaria.

PLATELETS IN MALARIA.

Lastly, the destructive action of hematin upon the platelets and the consequent tendency to hemorrhage is not without a parallel in malaria. The platelets are probably the only bodies in the blood whose numbers in malaria are influenced solely by the circulating toxin of the disease, and it is of especial significance, therefore, that the platelets are reduced both in malaria and in hematin intoxication. The tendency to hemorrhage produced by hematin has its counterpart in the well recognized class of hemorrhagic cases of pernicious malaria.

Here again the circulating hematin probably plays the important role in the production of the hemorrhagic condition. I do not wish to create the impression, however, that hemorrhages in malaria, or in hematin poisoning, are due solely to the destruction of platelets and prolongation of the bleeding time. This is certainly not the case in hematin poisoning in which profuse hemorrhage into the peritoneal cavity is of frequent occurrence in acutely fatal poisoning.

The pigment hematin must be regarded as an active factor in the production of many, if not all, of the important changes in the blood that characterize the various forms of malaria?

Modern methods of preventing malaria are explained and discussed editorially in The Lancet of London, published on June 28 last. The writer says:

Modern anti-malarial measures aim at the destruction of the insect host of the specific parasites and the prevention of the transference of the latter from one host to the other. The methods generally employed for the extermination of mosquitos are directed chiefly toward the abolition of their breeding places and the destruction of their eggs and larvae. It has been regarded by many persons as absolutely futile to attempt to extirpate the mature insect in infected localities, though it is admitted by others that some temporary benefit might, perhaps, follow the reduction of the number of mosquitos in a given area.

It cannot be denied that the abolition of mosquito breeding places often involves the construction of engineering or sanitary works which cause considerable expense. This question of expenditure has been put forward as one of the main arguments against the adoption of the modern scientific methods of malaria prophylaxis, and it is obvious that such outlay could hardly be justified in the case of small communities, and more particularly of temporary camps within malarious districts.

Our attention has been directed recently to this subject by an interesting paper published in our contemporary, The American Journal of Public Health (Vol. III., No. 2) by I. A. J. Orenstein, Assistant Chief Sanitary Inspector Isthmian Canal Commission. In this paper the value of 'mosquito catching' in dwellings as a prophylactic measure against malaria, more especially in temporary encampments, is emphasized, and a description is given of the methods which this expert employs to effect his purpose.

The various means used for killing mosquitos, anophelines and others, include an ordinary 'slapper' made of a six-inch square wire gauze; attached to a two-foot stick; a glass vial, such as is commonly employed by entomologists for collecting insects, containing a plug wetted with chloroform; and, lastly, a mosquito trap devised by a member of his staff. With this equipment the mosquito catcher passes from hut to hut. If the dwellings be screened the catching is done early in the morning and again in the evening. If the hut be not screened and the anophelines are abundant, search for them is made four or five times daily.

As proof of the success of his methods Dr. Orenstein quotes the results obtained by him in four camps situated in the jungle along the line of construction of the new Panama Railroad, where some 1,200 laborers were housed in 4 screened cars. Anophelines were very numerous, and but little could be done in the way of attacking the mosquito breeding places by which the camps were surrounded. By killing systematically day by day the mosquitos found within the huts in the manner above described it was found possible at a trivial cost to keep for a period of two or more years the malaria incidence rate in the camps practically as low as that of the remainder of the Canal Zone in which major works of drainage, oiling of pools, and other more or less expensive procedures had been carried out.

DESTROYING MOSQUITOS.

For the year 1910 the malaria incidence rate in the Canal Zone was 1.55 per cent, and in the four camps 1.53. The corresponding rates for 1911 were 1.54 and 1.84 respectively. The method described is said to be so simple that even a dull-witted West Indian negro laborer can be taught in a few days how to find and destroy the mosquitos in the huts. The expense involved was quite trivial, for the wage paid to the mosquito catchers was only 10 cents an hour, the lowest rate of remuneration paid to any class of worker in the Panama Canal Zone. The catching of the anophelines reduces the chances of attack upon the inmates of the houses, and the killing of mosquitos which have bitten an infected person before the plasmodia have had a chance to mature within the insect must tend to lessen greatly the risks of spreading the infection.

Dr. Orenstein says that when it is remembered that in malaria a period of at least one week must elapse before the mosquito which has fed upon an infected person can transmit the infection to another individual, and when it is also remembered that an anophellne filled with blood becomes sluggish and does not fly very far for some time, the efficacy of killing mosquitos in houses becomes self-evident. Where it is contemplated to carry out systematic anophelline catching in dwellings the interior walls should be painted a very light color so as to facilitate the work of the mosquito killer; and in dwellings which are dark some form of portable illumination must be carried by the person undertaking the duties of anophelline destroyer.

It cannot, we think, be denied that Dr. Orenstein's results are very satisfactory, but it is difficult to say how much of his success was, on the other hand, due to the screening of the huts in the four camps, and how much, on the other hand, was the result of the actual killing of the mosquitos found inside the extemporized dwellings occupied by the laborers in the swampy jungle of the Isthmus of Panama.

Malaria has been known in Greece and Italy for more than 2,000 years, says Dr. Ronald Ross in his classical work on "The Prevention of Malaria." Some scientists have attributed the downfall of Greece to the inroads made upon the health of the nation by malaria. It is well known that in both Greece and Italy sections that were populous and safely habitable gradually became malarial. It is supposed that the disease was introduced at the time of the first foreign expansion into both these countries.

Cinchona bark (from which quinine is derived) was introduced into Europe in 1640. The Countess d'El Cinchón, wife of the Viceroy of Peru, had been cured of a fever by means of it. She sent some of the remedy home, and it was named in honor of her.

The malarial parasite was discovered by H. Meckel in 1847.

Fighting Against Contagion in City

BY THE NEW YORK TIMES | NOV. 28, 1913

Modern methods, improved hospital personnel and application of science are keeping down the death rate.

IN ANNOUNCING A few days ago that hereafter "loose" milk of the grade sold in restaurants, soda-water fountains, lunch rooms, and hotels must be either pasteurized or certified, Health Commissioner Dr. Ernst J. Lederle pointed out as one reason for increased vigilance in watching the milk supply that during a recent typhoid fever epidemic on the east side the source of contagion for a whole district was found to be the milk sold "loose" in a certain store.

It is not generally known that the first actual provision for the hospital care and segregation of contagious disease in New York City was as late as 1853 when a hospital was built on Blackwell's Island. Since that time the work has grown, keeping pace with modern methods and increased learning. In the beginning of its hospital service the department found typhus to be the disease second in importance, so far as numbers were concerned, and first in importance in regard to death rate, with which it had to deal. The treatment in this disease was then, as now, purely symptomatic in character.

The one thing that the hospitals regarded as absolutely essential in preventing its spread was isolation and positive quarantine. The authorities worked upon a knowledge that the same measure that seemed to prevent the spread of smallpox seemed also to prevent the spread of typhus. The cause of the disease was unknown. It was not until the discovery was made of the way by which the disease could be transmitted that the sanitarian obtained knowledge which is effective in its control.

In 1885 the death rate from diphtheria was appalling and the treatment unsatisfactory. This year marked the beginning of the department work for the special care of diphtheria, scarlet fever, and measles cases. The Willard Parker Hospital was erected for the special care of diphtheria cases. In the latter disease various local applications in the form of antiseptics and the inhalation of the vaporized salt of mercury were employed, for the most part ineffectually.

Early in 1894 the reports of Von Behring, Roux, and Yersin suggested that a specific treatment for diphtheria would soon be available. Dr. Hermann M. Biggs, then director of the bacteriological laboratories of the Department of Health, visited the Institute for Infectious Diseases in Berlin, where Von Behring's experiments were being carried on, in the Summer of 1894. Dr. Biggs became convinced of the value of the new method in the treatment of diphtheria, and on his return presented a report to the board with a strong recommendation that an immediate appropriation be requested for the purpose of producing and using the new remedy.

The formal reports of the results of the treatment by Von Behring were not presented until October 1894, but the department was then already engaged in the inoculation of horses for the production of the serum, and on Jan. 1, 1895, the first active antitoxin produced in this country was available for use both in the hospitals of the Department of Health and in the tenement houses. The authorities say that the results obtained by the use of this remedy were wonderful. They are now a matter of general knowledge. The death rate in uncomplicated diphtheria which had formerly been very high is now practically negligible, when antitoxin is administered early in the disease.

It was in the hospital laboratory, now the Research Laboratory, on the grounds of the Willard Parker Hospital that the first high grade antitoxin was produced and it was in this same laboratory that the perfection of antitoxin by concentration and purification was first obtained. The Willard Parker Hospital for contagious diseases was therefore closely associated with these great advances in medical science.

In 1887, according to the Department Bulletin, Dr. O'Dwyer first published his article describing the operation of intubation, and it was in the hospitals of the Department of Health that it was most thoroughly demonstrated that this procedure was the means of saving many lives that otherwise would have been forfeited to larynigeal diphtheria.

The prevalence of broncho-pneumonia was so great in the Willard Parker Hospital in 1896 that the physicians in charge were forced to the belief that it was directly communicated from patient to patient. In an attempt to adopt measures of isolation a ward containing glass stalls was provided so that each patient, while in the same ward with others, was still separated from his neighbor. The results were so satisfactory that in a large percentage of the wards provided for contagious diseases this form of construction has been used.

Much experimental work of a research character has been carried on in the hospital laboratory in regard to the cause of measles. The actual cause of this disease, the authorities say, has never yet been ascertained, but in 1910 from blood obtained from a case Drs. Anderson and Goldberger of the Hygienic Laboratory at Washington were able to produce the disease in monkeys. The occurrence in the City of Washington of an epidemic of measles since this experiment gave opportunity to verify their findings, and another step toward the discovery of the cause of the disease was taken.

In the wards of the contagious disease hospitals every method of attacking scarlet fever that offered promise of discovery has been employed. In 1904 Dr. Mallory, following in the footsteps of Guarnieri's pathological researches involving the cornea of experimental animals, found in the skins of scarlet fever patient's bodies of a protozoan type, which he considered the cause of the disease. His work was repeated and a careful study made of patients in the scarlet fever hospital at the foot of East Sixteenth Street, but beyond the fact that the bodies were present in the skin, nothing further was proved.

When, in 1875, the Riverside Hospital was transferred from the Department of Charities and Correction to the Department of Health, the cases treated there were solely smallpox. At that time, the Bulletin points out, the treatment of this disease was primarily preventive, that is, it consisted in vaccination. The treatment of a developed case was purely symptomatic without any idea of curing the disease.

The Health Department Bulletin says:

After Pfeiffer's experiment which demonstrated the germicidal effect of a specific serum, it was thought that possibly there might be in the blood of animals recovering from vaccinia a specific serum which would produce the desired effect. In 1891 Dr. Erasmus Wilson, pathologist of the Kingston Avenue Hospital, then under the Department of Health of the City of Brooklyn, experimented with this method at the hospital and reported to the Board of Health of that city that he believed he had succeeded in modifying the course of a confluent case. Previous to the use of the serum, the prognosis had seemed absolutely hopeless, and, subsequent to its employment, the patient had made a rapid and complete recovery with considerably less than the usual amount of pitting.

At about this time this method of treatment was also in use in France, but the enormous amount of serum necessary (500 to 1,000 c. c.) precluded its general adoption. When Finsen reported the wonderful effects produced in lessening the pitting by the exclusion of the violet light rays, his method was adopted in the smallpox service of the contagious disease hospitals. Red panes of glass and red shades were provided in the smallpox wards. The results, however, were of a negative character.

During epidemics, considerable difficulty was formerly experienced in differentiating cases of variola (smallpox) from cases of varicella (chickenpox). In 1903, by inoculation with material furnished from the smallpox wards of Riverside Hospital, Dr. Park, the Director of the Research Laboratory then called the Hospital Laboratory, succeeded in producing the typical lesions of smallpox in monkeys. As these animals are known not to be susceptible to infection with the virus of chicken-pox, there was thus supplied an easy and ready method of confirming the diagnosis.

The department boasts that while better buildings and more improved methods of treatment were progressively employed in the hospital service, the personal service to the patients has also improved. In the beginning helpers of a low grade and "trusties" were in charge of the unfortunate victims of contagious diseases. A little later Sisters of Charity helped to raise the hospitals from this condition, and as soon as the services of specially trained nurses could be obtained they were employed. Now the term "pest house" is almost forgotten, and parents seek to have their children admitted to contagious disease hospitals that they may receive the benefit of the treatment, of long experience and leave their homes free from the dangers of infection.

Typhus, War's Dread Ally, Beaten

BY VAN BUREN THORNE, M.D. | APRIL 18, 1915

THE ANNOUNCEMENT OF the discovery of a protective vaccine against typhus fever, the dreadful scourge that dogs the heels of war, following closely upon the confirmation of the germ origin of the disease by repeated demonstrations of a distinct causative agent visible under the microscope, is but another instance of the accuracy of modern laboratory methods and the continual progress of medical science.

The concrete view of these achievements is that they could not have occurred at a more opportune moment in the history of the world. The stricken countries of Europe, already devastated by the wrath of man, are cowering beneath the brooding shadow of disease; and science, represented by the best and bravest of its exponents, is rushing from the four quarters of the earth the cumulative resources of a thousand laboratories to wage a war with Death.

The marvel of these two laboratory achievements is that they are the products of the labor of one so young. Dr. Harry Plotz of the Pathological Laboratory of Mount Sinai Hospital in this city is not yet 25 years old. He looks younger. It was strange, indeed, to listen to a youth unravel intricate problems of bacteriology in the presence of a gathering of distinguished pathologists at the Academy of Medicine on Wednesday evening last.

The discovery of the protective vaccine against typhus was made public at the same meeting at which the young bacteriologist told of the experimental labors of himself and his co-workers in isolating the bacillus of typhus fever.

While there has been no opportunity to demonstrate the efficiency of the vaccine in the presence of the disease itself, Dr. Plotz and his co-workers recommend its employment. And, in this connection, a high compliment already has been paid to the young discoverer: Dr. Hans Zinsser, the eminent Professor of Bacteriology of Columbia University, had himself inoculated with the protective vaccine before sailing on April 3 on his perilous mission as a member of the American Red Cross Sanitary Commission to cope with the epidemics of typhus in Serbia and Austria-Hungary.

The devotion of an entire evening by the New York Pathological Society (of which Professor Zinsser, by the way, is President) to the consideration of typhus fever, and particularly as to its origin, with Dr. Plotz as the central figure, cannot be regarded in any other light than as a distinct triumph for the Mount Sinai bacteriologist.

The first announcement of his discovery of the causative agent of typhus appeared in The New York Times on May 12, 1914. It was stated in the article that he would make public his discovery on the following day in a paper he was to read before the Association of American Physicians at Atlantic City. It was further made known in The Times that Dr. Plotz had determined as the result of the isolation of the germ that it was also the causative factor of the acute infectious ailment known as Brill's disease, which Dr. Nathan E. Brill of this city had classed as a distinctive malady. Dr. Plotz maintained that Brill's disease was in reality typhus fever of a mild type.

Dr. Plotz was present at the Atlantic City meeting, but his paper was not incorporated in the program. Neither was he called upon to address the gathering. No public reference was made by any physician present to typhus fever or its origin. When the writer of this article, who was present at the meeting, inquired of one of the officers of the association whether or not Dr. Plotz was to be invited to read his paper, the officer replied in the most emphatic manner:

"No such subject as the discovery of the typhus germ is to be discussed here."

Privately, the writer was informed by various physicians present that the young bacteriologist, just a year out of college, was not to read his paper for the simple reason that the news of his discovery had first been announced in a lay journal, namely, The New York Times.

It is fitting to emphasize here, however, the fact that Dr. Plotz did not furnish the news of his discovery to The Times, nor was he aware that this newspaper was in possession of the news until he saw it in print.

The meeting at the academy on Wednesday evening was the first public occasion, there, on which Dr. Plotz had an opportunity to discuss his work in the presence of a body of physicians best calculated to appraise its value. He was acclaimed by them as a scientific investigator of the first order.

Following his failure to be called upon at Atlantic City, Dr. Plotz prepared a brief preliminary paper, written in technical terms, in which he announced the isolation of an organism which occurred in typhus fever patients and which he believed to be the causative factor of the disease. He also obtained the same organism from patients suffering from Brill's disease. This paper appeared in the issue of The Journal of the American Medical Association, published on May 16, 1914.

The young scientist's paper of Wednesday proved to be an elaboration of his preliminary report, and contained a wealth of highly technical detail embodying the precise methods of isolating and cultivating pathogenic bacteria.

After identifying the typhus germ as the agent of Brill's disease, he discarded the term "Brill's disease," referring to it thereafter as endemic typhus as distinguished (and distinguishable by its milder clinical course) from the virulent and dreaded malady known as "European epidemic typhus," which already is said to have claimed 65,000 victims in Serbia, among them two heroic American physicians, and threatens to overrun the warring nations on the Continent, as well as their neutral neighbors.

If Dr. Plotz's findings relative to the identity of European epidemic typhus and Brill's disease are correct, and this is now vouched for by high authority, then we have typhus fever right here in New York, and have had sporadic cases for years. But the hygienic excellence of the systems of sanitation devised by the local health officers have ever prevented it from becoming a menace to the community. And it is now some twenty-six or twenty-eight years since a case of European typhus has had an opportunity to spread contagion in this city, thanks to the watchfulness of the Health Officers of the Port of New York.

It is true, however, that this ominous infection does sometimes reach our outposts at Quarantine, as Dr. Plotz related in his paper, for it was this very circumstance that enabled him to start an investigation into the origin of the disease. He learned of the presence of typhus patients removed from ships to the isolation hospitals in the lower bay from Dr. Joseph O'Connell, Health Officer of the Port, who permitted him to obtain blood specimens from these patients.

Dr. Plotz had formed an opinion as to the probable cause of typhus before submitting the blood of typhus patients to laboratory tests. This opinion was based on various theoretical considerations and on previous investigations. He considered it advisable to begin his search by looking for a so-called anaerobic organism as the causative agent of the acute infectious disease of unknown origin known as Brill's disease, and which owed its differentiation from other fevers, especially short-term typhoid fevers, to the keen clinical insight of Dr. Brill. An anaerobic organism is one which thrives best or thrives only when deprived of oxygen or air.

He used the anaerobic methods in examining the blood of six cases of Brill's disease, and isolated the same kind of bacillus from five of the six. He ascribes his failure in the sixth instance to the fact that the blood was not taken from the patient until after the crisis of the disease had passed. Subsequent investigation disclosed the fact that the bacillus is present in the blood when the fever is at its height, but disappears after the crisis.

Other investigators have isolated various micro-organisms from cases of typhus and Brill's disease, but none of them resembled that obtained by Dr. Plotz nor were they constantly present. The Plotz bacillus is constant in both its presence and appearance.

It is also true that in recent years other investigators have declared that Brill's disease is probably a mild or modified typhus. Some two or three years ago a discussion was carried on between two or three medical officers of the United States Government and Dr. Brill relative to the nature of the disease, the Federal physicians maintaining that it was typhus fever.

In accordance with the same belief and after having isolated the bacillus from the cases of Brill's disease, Dr. Plotz took specimens of blood from half a dozen patients suffering from European epidemic typhus in the hospitals at Quarantine, the patients having been removed from transatlantic vessels, and subjected the blood to bacteriological tests in the Mount Sinai laboratories. His co-workers were Dr. George Baehr, like himself a graduate of the College of Physicians and Surgeons of Columbia University, and Dr. Peter K. Olitzky, a graduate of the Medical College of Cornell University.

From all of the typhus cases Dr. Plotz was able to recover a micro-organism apparently identical with that isolated from the cases of Brill's disease.

In order to check up or verify this discovery, the blood of 198 control cases (that is, cases in which typhus fever or Brill's disease were not present, but in which other diseases such as influenza were diagnosed) was treated and examined in exactly the same manner, but the bacillus was not found in any specimen.

The evidence indicated that the virus was present in the blood during the febrile period of the disease, that it was non-filterable and hence most likely of microscopic size, and that it was of bacterial rather than of protozoal origin. Subjected to microscopical examination, the agent was seen to be a small bacillus, pleomorphic, or occurring in more than one form, varying from nine-tenths to 1.93 microns in length, the breadth being from one-fifth to three-fifths of the length.

When first isolated, Dr. Plotz says in his paper, the organism grows only anaerobically, or without air or oxygen, but after a time it can be grown aerobically, or in the presence of air.

During the febrile period of the disease, the organism was yielded from the blood in 100 per cent of typhus fever cases. The blood of thirty-seven patients suffering from the endemic type, heretofore known as Brill's disease, the cultures of which were examined at various times, yielded the bacillus in 53 per cent of cases.

From a pure culture of the bacillus, inoculations were made into the peritoneal cavities of two guinea pigs. The incubation period of the infection proved to be from twenty-four to forty-eight hours, for within that period there was a rise of temperature, which remained high for four or five days, and which dropped rapidly by crisis.

This clinical picture corresponded exactly with the result obtained in guinea pips inoculated with the blood of typhus fever patients, with the single exception that the incubation period is shorter.

It was proved also that serum from a convalescing typhus fever patient had bactericidal action against the organism obtained from both Brill's disease and European epidemic typhus.

This paragraph ended Dr. Plotz's preliminary report:

In a later communication it is proposed to consider the cultural charac-teristics of the organism, its agglutination reactions, the further results of animal experiments, and cross-immunity tests. At the same time the results of studies forming a basis for a possible vaccine prophylaxis and comparative studies of other organisms described by various authors as being found in typhus fever will be reported.

This promised elaboration was given in detail on Wednesday evening, and the vaccine prophylaxis hinted at in the earlier com-munication resulted in the journey of Professor Zinsser and his fellow-scientists to the stricken fields of Europe after inoculation with an agent which it is hoped will prove effective against the acquisition of the infection.

Those who sailed with Professor Zinsser on the expedition, financed by the Red Cross and the Rockefeller Foundation, are Dr. Thomas W. Jackson of Philadelphia, Dr. Andrew W. Sellarde, Dr. George C. Shattuck, and Dr. Francis B. Grinnell of the Harvard Med-ical School; Dr. F. W. Caldwell, Hobart D. Brink, W. S. Standifer, and Luis de la Pena.

The two latter were members of the staff of General William C. Gorgas in the sanitary campaign in the Panama Canal Zone. Dr. Nicolle, the French expert on typhus, has been invited to cooperate with the commission.

The members of the expedition will meet in Saloniki, and proceed to the districts of Austria-Hungary which are stricken with epidemics of typhus, cholera, and other contagious diseases.

When the Rockefeller expedition was projected Dr. Richard P. Strong, Professor of Tropical Diseases at the Harvard Medical School, was appointed leader. He is already in Europe. More recently, however, announcement has been made that General Gorgas, Surgeon General of the United States Army, the world's foremost sanitarian, is to proceed to Serbia to assume charge of the commission.

Prior to the announcement of the proposal to have General Gorgas take charge of the work, he stated that he believed the commission would win the fight against disease in Serbia. He characterized the expedition as the most efficient ever organized in the history of modern sanitation.

Dr. Samuel Taylor Darling, the bacteriologist who was associated with General Gorgas in the Canal Zone, arrived here from Colon on Tuesday. It is reported that he will accompany his former chief to Serbia. He went to South Africa in 1933 with General Gorgas when the latter was invited to go there by the Rand mine owners to see what could be done to lessen the mortality among miners.

Now, as to the disease typhus fever itself. The fact has been established that the infection is communicated from one to another by a carrier, namely, the body louse. Hence it is that the disease becomes epidemic in places where large numbers are crowded together under insanitary conditions. It is the invariable sequel of prolonged warfare where large numbers are wounded.

The disease has broken out under various conditions other than warfare as an epidemic — for example, in prisons, on shipboard, and in hospitals. Hence it has been called prison or jail fever, hospital fever, and ship's fever. It has also been known as spotted fever.

Clinically, typhus is marked by a high temperature, great mental and physical depression, and skin eruptions. It lasts for about two weeks. There are no specific lesions, except enlargement of the spleen. It seems to be disappearing in those centres where municipal hygiene is making steady advances.

Dr. Plotz received a real ovation at the conclusion of his paper on Wednesday evening from the 250 or more physicians assembled. He ended by announcing that Dr. William H. Welch, the distinguished head of the medical department of Johns Hopkins University, had christened the newly discovered germ of typhus. It is called bacillus typhii exanthematus.

Among those present were some of the world's foremost medical investigators, and following the reading of two papers bearing on Dr. Plotz's discoveries by his co-workers, Dr. Olitzky and Dr. Baehr, he was the recipient of public congratulations from them. The first one called upon to express his opinion of the work was Dr. Hideyo Noguchi, a famous laboratory worker, attached to the staff of the Rockefeller Institute for Medical Research.

"I believe it must now appear to any person," said Dr. Noguchi, "that the organism has been isolated. I congratulate the three physicians on showing the problem of the cause of one of the most mysterious diseases of which we know anything."

Dr. William Hallock Park, noted as a bacteriologist, and head of the Bacteriological Department of the Board of Health of this city, said:

"Dr. Plotz had the mind and the will to do this work, and he has carried it to a successful conclusion."

Dr. Nathan E. Brill, the discoverer of Brill's disease, ungrudgingly admitted that at last it had been demonstrated beyond question that Brill's disease and typhus are identical, differing only in degree of severity.

"This discovery is a particular gratification to me," said he warmly. "This is the first work which has established the absolute identity of the two types of the disease.

"I long ago admitted that they were related, but I contended that this had not been established by the work of Anderson and Goldberger. I admitted the relationship, but denied the identity — which is now established beyond dispute. I doubt, however, the statement that the louse is the only means of communicating the disease from one to another."

"I congratulate these gentlemen," said Dr. Samuel J. Meltzer of the Rockefeller Institute, famous in many fields of medical research, "not only on the way in which they carried on their investigations, but on the manner in which they have presented them to us."

"Mention has been made of the fact that a vaccine has been made," said Dr. K. S. Mandelbaum of the Mount Sinai Hospital staff. "Some of the members of the commission on the way to fight typhus in Serbia, and others who intend to go, have already been inoculated with the vaccine — of course, without any guarantee of its efficacy. They came to us and asked to be inoculated."

Dr. E. Libman, also of the Mount Sinai staff, interjected a touch of the romance of science into his remarks.

"This discovery was no chance observation," he said. "Plotz was worried about Brill's disease when a student. He took the position at Mount Sinai after graduation on purpose to find out the cause of Brill's disease. He found the organism the first time he tried for it."

Dr. Plotz, whose discoveries may mitigate the menace of typhus, was born in Paterson, N. J., in 1890. He attended the schools in Newark, and for a time was a pupil at the Boys' High School in Brooklyn. Later he entered Columbia University and took a combination course which gave him his academic degree from Columbia College and his medical degree from the College of Physicians and Surgeons. He was graduated in 1913, at the head of his class. Upon his graduation he took a competitive examination for pathological interne at Mount Sinai Hospital, and was first among 200 contestants.

Find Sun Produces the 4th Vitamine

BY THE NEW YORK TIMES | JUNE 20, 1922

WHILE THE STUDY of rickets at Johns Hopkins University has resulted in the discovery reported yesterday of a fourth type of vitamin (Vitamin D), the study of rickets at the College of Physicians and Surgeons of Columbia University has indicated that sunlight may produce vitamins directly in the human blood.

The experiments at the College of Physicians and Surgeons indicated that the frequent exposure of the skin of a child to the direct rays of the sun cured rickets without any change of diet. Copious use of cod liver oil also cured rickets.

Cod liver oil is the richest of substances in the mysterious unidentified objects called vitamins, and its vitamins have commonly been supposed to be the agent which cures the rickets. Sunlight, however, according to the New York experiments, does exactly what cod liver oil does. No definite claim has been made as to the manner in which the sunlight acts, whether it produces new vitamins or increases the activity of those already in existence in the patient or operates in some other way, but X-ray photographs and blood analyses are said to corroborate fully the assertion that the sunlight produces direct chemical changes in the blood, restoring the impaired bones steadily until a complete cure is effected.

The effects of sunlight in the cure of rickety children has been confirmed, according to medical reports by Dr. Alfred F. Hess of the College of Physicians and Surgeons, by experiments on animals. Numbers of rats have been fed on diets which produce rickets. The disease has inevitably appeared in those kept in darkness. It has been invariably prevented in those regularly kept in the sun.

The blood analysis of patients has again confirmed the mysterious effect of sunlight on the blood. Rickets results when something goes wrong with the bone-building process in children. The amount of phosphorus in the blood is always found to be below normal in those afflicted by the rickets. Without any change of diet, the sunlight produces from day to day a steady increase in the amount of inorganic phosphorus in the blood. This effect is believed to be due to the penetration of the ultra-violet rays of the sun through the skin and by its production of some kind of chemical reaction in the blood-stream.

Deficiency of fresh vegetables is one of the chief faults in diet which cause rickets, but the disease may appear in children regardless of diet.

Two further reasons for considering lack of sunlight as a cause are the greater prevalence of the disease in large cities where smoke or the heights of buildings cut off sunlight and the fact that the disease occurs chiefly in Winter, when there is less sunlight.

The treatment of rickety infants involves exposure of their arms and legs and body to the sunlight for regular periods each day. The exposure is direct, because if the light passes through glass a large part of the ultra-violet rays may be absorbed. Cod liver oil or sunlight in sufficient quantities are a perfect cure for rickets, according to Dr. Hess. According to his estimate $50,000 worth of cod liver oil would be sufficient to cure all of the cases of the disease in the City of New York.

The discovery that sunlight has a very active chemical effect on the blood has caused further interest, because of the possibility that the absence of that effect may produce other diseases than rickets and may be a contributing factor to various complaints.

The discovery of a vitamin in meats by the Department of Agriculture reported yesterday is also paralleled, it was learned, by work done at Columbia University, in investigating the statements of Vilhjalmur Stefansson, the explorer, who reported that his experiences in the Arctic proved that fresh meat of any kind whatsoever would prevent or cure scurvy. That fresh vegetables would cure scurvy was well known, but that fresh meat would have any such effect was disputed.

Serum Proves Boon in Fighting Diabetes

BY THE NEW YORK TIMES | OCT. 8, 1922

EXPERIMENTS IN THE treatment of diabetes, hitherto regarded as practically incurable, have met with remarkable success, according to reports by officials of the Carnegie Corporation, which has made an appropriation for research work at the Potter Metabolic Laboratory and Clinic in California. The treatment that is being administered has given relief in practically all the cases under observation.

The ravages of the disease have been checked by application of a serum discovered by Canadian physicians working under Dr. J. J. R. Macleod of the University of Toronto. This serum has been used at the Potter laboratory. Thus far relief has been dependent upon constant application of the serum. It is too early, physicians say, to describe the treatment as a "sure cure" for diabetes, for the experiments at the Potter laboratory have been going on for only about eighteen months.

Dr. Henry S. Pritchett, President of the Carnegie Corporation, who recently visited the Potter clinic and observed the experiments there, has made a report on the study and treatment there of diabetes, for incorporation in the annual report of the corporation.

DR. POTTER FIRST STARTED WORK.

Dr. Potter's metabolic research began at the French Hospital here. He removed to Santa Barbara, Cal., where a metabolic clinic and laboratory was built by public-spirited Californians. The Carnegie Corporation has aided the work by an annual appropriation. Dr. Potter died in 1919, and since then the work has been carried on under the direction of W. D. Sansum.

Intensive studies on the internal secretion of the pancreas had been carried on in the meantime under Dr. Macleod in Canada. It has long been known that some pathology of the pancreas is responsible for diabetes. Dr. F. G. Banting, working under Dr. Macleod, carried on intensive experiments to extract a substance from pancreatic tissues. This substance was first injected into dogs suffering with diabetes. The diabetic symptoms disappeared with the application of the serum, which is known as insulin. Convincing results of the efficacy of the serum were obtained by Dr. Banting in the cases of humans suffering with the disease.

"On account of the admirable facilities in the Potter Metabolic Clinic in Santa Barbara and the opportunity afforded by the close association of laboratory and hospital," Dr. Pritchett's report says, "Dr. Macleod and his associates most generously and kindly communicated to Dr. Sansum and his staff in Santa Barbara such full information as they had and because of the urgent heed for such an extract of the pancreas urged their immediate co-operation. With the information thus generously given through Dr. Macleod, the staff of the Potter Metabolic Clinic began strenuous efforts in the insolation of the internal secretion of the pancreas now known as insulin. They were immediately successful and within two months had been able to secure a sufficient amount of insulin to use on nine severe cases of diabetes."

SUCCESS OF TREATMENT ESTABLISHED.

The results have been so convincing that there can be no doubt of the great value of this substance in the treatment of diabetes and it is quite within the possibilities that the discovery may result in the relief and cure of great numbers of people from this scourge. The following cases will illustrate the extraordinary sort of results which have been obtained:

> *A patient of 53 years of age was sent to the clinic on the verge of diabetic coma, apparently death within a few days awaited him. Following the administration of insulin he became immediately free from sugar, his diet could be increased to normal and he is rapidly gaining in strength and weight.*

A boy of 12 in extreme illness through diabetes became free from sugar after twenty-four hours of treatment with insulin has remained free although his diet has been increased to practically normal. This boy is gaining weight at the rate of half a pound a day and is leading the type of life that any normal active child would lead. By the older dietary methods partial starvation would have been necessary even to prolong life, to say nothing of restoration to health. The results in the other cases have been equally astonishing.

EXPENSE OF SERUM IS VERY GREAT.

The problem is of course still in its infancy. Insulin is prepared at present at very great expense. Cheaper methods of production must be devised. A study of the intricate chemistry of the product will undoubtedly add materially to our knowledge of the oxidative processes going on in the body about which practically nothing is known at present. But the great gains seem to be that patients with the use of this new agent will not only be able to be sugar free, but will be able to have normal diets with the strength and health which can come alone from the use of such food.

The brilliant success which has come from this study and the still more brilliant prospects of the future which it holds out form a source of the greatest encouragement to the trustees of the corporation that their gifts may, if given with discretion, advance the cause of medical knowledge and thereby increase human happiness and usefulness in the most desirable fashion. Mr. Carnegie had always in mind the desire to 'find the efficient man and enable him to do his work.' Not every research can show the brilliant results which have come out of these investigations, but all patient, long-continued study adds, little by little, to the sum of knowledge, enriches life, and helps to turn away misfortune.

Not the least pleasing feature of this investigation lies in the generous and admirable attitude in which two sets of investigators, each of whom has received modest help from the Carnegie Corporation, have co-operated toward their common end. It was a graceful and generous act on the part of Dr. Macleod and his colleagues to put at the service of the Potter Metabolic Clinic the full results of their important researches, but this action is in entire consonance with the spirit and the purpose of true scientific research.

Finds New Remedy for Pneumonia

BY THE NEW YORK TIMES | MAY 9, 1924

Dr. L. B. Felton, Harvard, after 5 years' research, isolates antibody that kills germ.

ANNOUNCEMENT WAS MADE yesterday in Boston and in this city that Dr. Lloyd B. Felton of the Department of Preventive Medicine and Hygiene at Harvard Medical School had found a treatment for pneumonia which is expected to cut the death rate from that disease by 25 or 50 per cent.

The announcement was made with the authority of Dr. Milton J. Rosenau of Harvard, Dr. William H. Park and other conservative medical men after the remedy had been found remarkably successful in sixty pneumonia cases treated in Boston and sixty treated in this city by Dr. Park and others.

The substance discovered by Dr. Felton is a white crystalline powder which he has separated from the ordinary horse serum that has been used with uncertain results in the treatment of pneumonia. This white crystalline powder is believed to be the protective substance or the antibody against pneumonia in a pure, or a nearly pure, state.

USED ON 120 HUMAN PATIENTS.

This substance has now been injected into 120 human cases without the slightest unfavorable reaction. It is apparently entirely clear from the elements which in the horse serum have caused chills, fever and the so-called "serum sickness." The unpurified serum has caused such violent reactions that many physicians discarded it after some experience with its results.

The discovery was an outgrowth of five years of work, organized by the Metropolitan Life Insurance Company of this city after the influenza epidemic of 1918. This company brought together many leading research workers in the field of pneumonia and influenza and financed research. These specialists, who formed what was known as the Influenza Commission of the Metropolitan Life Insurance Company, met regularly and frequently.

As regards influenza the five years' work has been barren of positive accomplishment but many delusions about the disease have been swept aside. The very existence of Pfeiffer's bacillus, which was the supposed cause of influenza, was discredited. The investigators demonstrated that the immunity caused by anti-influenza vaccines was brief and feeble and that such vaccines did not give protection against pneumonia.

VALUABLE IN FIGHT ON INFLUENZA.

While no direct progress has been made against influenza, Dr. Felton's discovery is of immense importance in the fight against influenza, because the pernicious thing about influenza has been that it brought on pneumonia. According to some investigators influenza never directly caused death, but produced its mortality solely by paving the way for pneumonia.

Pneumonia causes an average of 90,000 deaths a year in this country, hence Dr. Felton's discovery has the potential power, according to yesterday's announcement, of saving between 22,500 and 45,000 lives each year. It was hinted that the pure antibody powder produced by Dr. Felton may have an efficacy greater than 50 per cent in treating these cases.

Dr. Felton described what he had done in a paper which was read before the New England Health Association at Boston. This was a highly scientific document giving each step of his researches. The announcement, with more detail about the results achieved in many cases, was made in this city by Lee K. Frankel, Second Vice President of the Metropolitan Life Insurance Company.

DISCOVERER 32 YEARS OLD.

Dr. Felton is 32 years old. He was born at Pinegrove Mills, Pa., spent most of his youth in New Philadelphia, Ohio, and was graduated in 1916 from Johns Hopkins. He went to Harvard in the Fall of 1922, where he has been working constantly under Dr. Milton J. Rosenau on problems concerning the "mechanism" of the antibody action which causes unknown substances in certain serums to aid in the destruction of disease germs.

Taking the serum from horses into which large numbers of pneumococci had been injected, Dr. Felton filtered it, sought in various ways to obtain precipitates from it, treated it chemically and electrically — always with the hope of forcing the crude serum to give up the specific substance that attacked the pneumococcus, or pneumonia germ.

It was well-known that injections of pneumococcus caused the horse to develop in its blood a substance that aided in destroying or digesting the germ. This substance — the so-called antibody — was known to be carried in the serum, or clear liquid of the blood. The problem was to obtain the pure antibodies, or a high concentrate of them, so that it no longer would be necessary to inject the highly diluted horse serum with its injurious by-products into the human being. The antibodies existed in quantities so minute that a large dose of serum was necessary to have an effect on pneumonia in a human patient; and a dose of the necessary proportions was regarded by many as worse than the disease.

ISOLATION OF SUBSTANCE SIMPLE.

The process of isolating, or virtually isolating, the antibodies was found to be simple. After all kinds of elaborate chemical and physical processes had been used without notable success, Dr. Felton became interested in a white fluffy substance that appeared when the serum from a treated horse was mixed with water in the proportion of ten parts of water to one of serum. Collecting and purifying the white fluff, he found that it dried into a white crystalline powder which he suspected of containing the antibodies in a highly concentrated form.

The substance was first tested in vivisection experiments on great numbers of mice. Groups of mice received injections of pneumonia germs. Half of them later received the white powder — and recovered. All those not so treated died.

Quantities of germs sufficient to kill a million mice were injected into one mouse. After a time the white powder was shot into it. Recovery followed.

This left no doubt that Dr. Felton had discovered something that had specific and remarkably potent properties for killing pneumonia germs outright or for exciting the white corpuscles to digest and destroy the germs.

It was only after prolonged experimentation with mice that the white powder was used on human patients.

SENT TO VARIOUS HOSPITALS.

After exact measurements of the potency of the substance to ascertain the dose needed, the powder was distributed to hospitals in Boston, New York and Brooklyn. The injection is made directly into the vein. After its trial in human cases, Dr. Rosenau said:

> *I believe a distinct advance has been made in the treatment of pneumonia. The antibody solution has a potent power in preventing and even curing pneumococcic infection in susceptible animals. It is beneficial in lobar pneumonia of man.*
>
> *Before the final word can be said concerning the usefulness and also the limitations of this agent, much scientific work must be done and the experience of clinicians in different places at all seasons of the year must be collected and studied.*

The work of Dr. Felton may bear fruit in many other ways. In isolating antibodies, or in obtaining them in high concentration, he has made an advance which may be useful in developing treatments for other diseases. The antibody has been an almost complete mystery, and the Harvard investigator has succeeded in partly lifting the curtain on it. From his researches it is said to be highly probable that a technique will be developed that may increase the efficacy of serums for other diseases than pneumonia and may make it possible to use concentrated antibodies for treatment in some infectious diseases, where the serum cannot now be used successfully.

GENERAL BACTERIA LAW REPRESENTED.

"In addition to pneumococci, as a matter of control, it has been found possible," Dr. Felton said in his paper, "to isolate the protective substance in immune sera developed by other micro-organisms. There are indications that the protective antibody of the pneumococcus is one of many which act in similar fashion, and its behavior represents a general law for certain groups of bacteria."

The results announced concern Type I. of pneumonia, the type responsible for most of the deaths from this disease. Dr. Felton reported, however, that he had succeeded in isolating the protective substance in Types II. and III. Their use had not advanced to a stage, however, when they could be announced as specific remedies for those types of pneumonia.

When the white substance was first obtained by diluting the serum with water, it was tried on horses and found to confer a high degree of immunity against the pneumococci. After treatment in various ways the sera taken from different horses was re-tested for the white precipitate and the results gave an interesting cross-reference on the efficacy of the serum.

"Two significant facts were developed by the experiment," said Dr. Felton, "first, that the amount of precipitate appears to indicate the degree of protective power of the serum; and second, that the precipitable substance disappears from the serum of a horse as the protective power of the serum is lost."

EASY TO MAKE IN LARGE LOTS.

Only a small quantity of the antibody concentrate has been produced so far, but the process of obtaining it is so simple, according to Dr. Frankel, that it can be manufactured in large quantities, if there is a large demand for it.

The discovery of insulin, for instance, caused severe embarrassment to hundreds of practitioners, because thousands of diabetic patients demanded the insulin treatment at a time when insulin was being produced only in laboratory quantities. It was a year before short-cuts in production had been achieved which enabled the supply of insulin to catch up with the demand.

The method of producing the antipneumonia concentrate from large quantities of serum was described as follows by Dr. Felton:

> One liter of serum was slowly poured into fifteen liters of agitated, cool, distilled water and the precipitate allowed to settle overnight in the icebox or cold-room. The clear, supernatant fluid was siphoned off and the flocculent precipitate was washed with the same volume of cool, distilled water used for the precipitation, the mixture being well agitated. The suspension was permitted to settle during another twenty-four-hour period. Again the supernatant liquid was siphoned off and the white substance collected by means of a Sharples centrifuge. The compact white residue in the bowl of the Sharples was taken out and dissolved in one-half molecular sodium chlorid. If the solution was not clear, clarification was obtained in the Sharples and it was then passed through a Berkefeld candle. With two of the lots, the substance, after being suspended in wash water, failed to settle.

ANTIBODY CLASSED AS A GLOBULIN.

After a highly technical discussion, Dr. Felton told of steps taken to find out the chemical constitution of the antibody.

> For the purpose of purification and qualitative tests," he said, "a sample of the precipitate was washed in water, redissolved in sodium chlorid and precipitated five separate times. The resultant product was a white fluffy substance almost entirely insoluble in water but readily soluble in dilute acids and alkaline and in most natural salts.
>
> This well-washed substance gives a positive reaction to all the common protein tests. It contains phosphorus and sulphur. The heat coagulation point when dissolved in sodium chlorid is 70 degrees Centigrade. These tests show that the protective substance is classed as a globulin, but it must not be inferred that its protective power is necessarily the entire globulin structure.

The next tests were to discover whether the antibody for Type I. gave it protection against Type II. and Type III. of pneumonia.

"These results indicate," said Dr. Felton. "that there is some cross-protection with this single lot of antibody solution. The degree of protection is slight when compared to its effects on Type I. organisms, and it is only present in some of the strains tested."

Under the head of "Mechanism of Action" Dr. Felton proceeded to discuss experiments intended to discover how the protective substance accomplished its work. It was found to have a definite bactericidal action — that is, it killed the germs outright to some extent.

Then it was found that in blood in the living animal and in blood in the test tube, the addition of a certain amount of the antibody solution caused more energetic action by the white corpuscles in destroying the pneumococcus. Dr. Felton said there appeared to be no parallelism between the bactericidal action of the substance and its power to confer immunity.

After a discussion of the size of dosage and the measurement of immunity. Dr. Felton continued:

> Practically all efforts in this study have been limited to: Type I. serum of high potency. However, a sufficient number of experiments have been made on Type II. and III. sera to show definitely that the antibody solution can be prepared from them. The main difficulty has been in obtaining immune sera for these two types of sufficiently high protective power to make experimentation feasible.
>
> The obstacle, in part, has been overcome by first dialyzing the serum to reduce the inorganic content and subsequently diluting the dialyzed material in a dilute phosphate buffer.
>
> The success with any of the types is commensurable with the degree of immunity obtained in the horse, or the amount of antibody in serum. It is not improbable that, since we have a definite substance for which to seek, modification can be made in our methods of immunization that will enable the preparation of the antibody for one type just as readily as for another.

METROPOLITAN LIFE'S STATEMENT.

In its statement announcing the discovery the Metropolitan Life Insurance Company said:

> The value of the discovery to mankind cannot yet be measured. None of the scientists has sufficient data yet to make more than an estimate, and yet the most skeptical of those familiar with Dr. Felton's work admit that at least a 25 per cent, and possibly a 50 per cent, reduction in pneumonia mortality is assured.
>
> The supreme simplicity of the discovery of the precipitation of the serum in water gives the layman a false impression as to the duration and character of the work leading up to the discovery and essential before it could be made. The discovery was in no sense a lucky accident. Even the apparatus required for the work is of extraordinary intricacy and required lengthy studies and experimentation to develop.
>
> 'Even if the serum has no increased potency by the concentration, the fact that serum sickness has been eliminated revolutionizes the treatment of pneumonia,' one physician pointed out. 'General practitioners had practically given up the use of pneumonia serum because of the insurmountable difficulties. This will put it back into common practice.'

GREAT STRIDES ARE FORECAST.

> The discovery is in many ways a parallel to the concentration and refinement of diphtheria antitoxin. It is predicted that the great strides made in the prevention and cure of diphtheria will be duplicated to a considerable extent during the next decade in the fight on pneumonia.
>
> The members of the Influenza Commission of the Metropolitan Life Insurance Company, which fostered and financed the work, are, in addition to Doctors Rosenau and Dr. Park, Dr. W. H. Frost, Professor of Epidemiology and Public Health Administration, Johns Hopkins School of Hygiene and Public Health, Baltimore; Dr. G. W. McCoy, director of the Hygienic Laboratory, Washington; Dr. E. O. Jordan, Professor of Hygiene and Bacteriology, University of Chicago; Dr. Lee K. Frankel, Second Vice President of the Metropolitan, and Dr. A. S. Knight, medical director of the Metropolitan.
>
> Dr. Felton's discovery is only one of the long and patient researches of the members of the commission working in five laboratories in various parts of the country over a period of five years.

Serum Discovered for Scarlet Fever by Long Research

BY THE NEW YORK TIMES | JAN. 17, 1924

DR. A. R. DOCHEZ, Associate Professor of Medicine at the College of Physicians and Surgeons, Columbia University, and visiting physician at the Presbyterian Hospital, announced last night at the 139th meeting of the Society for Experimental Biology and Medicine, Cornell University Medical College, the discovery of a serum for scarlet fever.

In carefully worded phrases, admittedly designed to prevent the medical and lay world from jumping to conclusions that he had a panacea. Dr. Dochez said there were no grounds yet for stating that the serum is a definitive curative agent, but in a limited number of cases dealt with at New Haven Hospital by Dr. Francis G. Blake, Professor of Medicine at Yale University School of Medicine, "certain promise" had been shown.

Dr. Dochez's address before a small body of scientists, biologists, surgeons and physicians was headed "Studies Concerning the Significance of Streptococcuc Hemolytlcus." Under this technical title he traced the developments which led him to believe that this microorganism was responsible for scarlet fever and how Dr. Blake had apparently successfully used a serum from horses immunized by the streptococcus in question.

SUSPECTED FORTY YEARS.

"The relation of streptococcus hemolyticus to scarlet fever has been under discussion for the past forty years," said Dr. Dochez.

The more or less constant pressure of this micro-organism in the throats of individuals suffering from that disease has been generally recognized. This organism is also the preponderant causative agent of such septic complications of the malady as interstitial nephritis, arthritis and septicemia, and is present in many infections, such as sore throat, erysipelas and various abscesses.

Such widespread and general relationship of streptococcus to scarlet fever naturally gave rise to the view supported by a number of investigators that streptococcus might be the etiological agent of the disease. Belief in the validity of this conception led to the preparation and trial of anti-streptococci sera for therapeutic purposes.

On the other hand, another group of investigators have asserted that streptococcus bears only a secondary relationship to scarlet fever and cannot be assigned the principal causative role. Discussion of this question was carried on for many years and became part of the larger controversy concerning the nature of the whole group of organisms generally designated the streptococcus hemolyticus.

Finally, however, the balance was tipped against the etiological importance of this organism by Professor Jochmann, who claimed that it was unreasonable to suppose that such a disease as scarlet fever could be caused by an organism giving rise to such varied manifestations as this one, and furthermore that the presence of this organism could not be demonstrated in certain rapidly fatal malignant instances of the disease.

AGAIN ON GERM'S TRAIL.

It was held, therefore, until the last four years or so that scarlet fever was caused by an unknown virus. More recent research work, however, tended to show that this streptococcus was the cause of the disease, and after a series of complicated biological experiments extending over a period of several years fresh evidence pointing this way was obtained.

In 1919 a technic for the differentiation of biological types of S. hemolyticus was developed. This discovery led to a re-examination of the type of streptococcus associated with scarlet fever. As a result of these studies, it was found by several investigators that the type of hemolytic streptococcus found in the throats of scarlet fever patients is in general a specific type readily distinguished from the types of the same organism causing other kinds of septic conditions in general. Furthermore, this specific streptococcus has been isolated from the local wound in wound scarlet fever, from the infected burn in burn scarlet fever and from milk contaminated with the illness.

More careful study of the throat secretions of scarlet fever patients has demonstrated the organism to be present at some time during the disease in 100 per cent of instances. It would seem, therefore, that the two main objections of Jochmann to the etiological significance of hemolytieus in scarlet fever has been answered. As a result of these studies the question again assumes renewed importance.

Ever since the institution of these studies we have made more or less continued efforts to produce in animals with a scarletinal type of S. hemolytieus a disease resembling scarlet fever. At first these efforts met with questionable success. More recently with a special technic we have been more successful and have produced in guinea pigs a condition resembling in its main features certain of the phenomena of scarlet fever.

The animals develop fever, a temporary increase in the white corpuscles of the blood, lose weight, and on the second and third days show a transient rash. On the eighth to the twelfth day general disquamation appears most conspicuously on the pads of the feet.

IMMUNIZE A HORSE.

In view of the similarity to scarlet fever of the symptom complex produced in guinea pigs we decided to immunize a horse by a similar procedure.

We have recently obtained from this horse an immune serum, which has been tested for its capacity to materialize the rash locally in the skin in the human cases of scarlet fever. In all the cases tested so far a positive neutralization has recurred, which is somewhat more conspicuous than that obtained under similar circumstance from the use of scarletinal sera from patients in a convalescent state. We propose in the near future to test the serum therapeutically. It would seem that the disease may not be unlike diphtheria, in that the principal localization of the infection is in the throat, where the organism produces a toxin which gives rise to the general symptoms and the rash.

Dr. Blake at New Haven Hospital was asked to conduct further researches with the horse serum. He has reported that after a period it was found the serum produced the same effects in scarlet fever patients as a serum from recovered cases of the disease. That is to say, patches of the skin were cleared from the rash. I wish to emphasize again that, though Dr. Blake reports certain promise in a limited number of cases,

Rockefeller Institute for Medical Research.

*there are no grounds as yet for stating that a serum has been discovered
which is a definitive curative agent. I do this in order to prevent any mis-
apprehension, for when such discoveries have been previously announced
both the medical world and the public have, often unnecessarily, been
thrown into a fever heat?*

RESEARCH GOES ON HERE, TOO.

It was learned last night from an authoritative medical source that
research work with the scarlet fever serum has been actively conducted
at the Rockefeller Institute for Medical Research, Avenue A and East
Sixty-sixth Street, and in the laboratories of the Presbyterian Hospital.
Further research work will be carried on both at these two institutions
and at New Haven Hospital. Those who are interested in the matter hope
at a later date to be in a position to make a more definite announcement.

It was also pointed out that it is but one step from a serum to vaccine, and, therefore there was every hope that within the near future

there would be for scarlet fever not only a curative but preventive agent.

Recent statistics show that in the United States there are about 100,000 cases of scarlet fever annually. In New York the average is about 100 a week. Scarlet fever is a Spring disease and in the months from February to April, statistics show, the cases run sometimes as high as 300 weekly in this city. The average mortality is between 3 and 4 per cent, but the malady, like many other infectious diseases, comes in waves of varying intensity and there have been periods when the mortality rose to 13 per cent. It attacks chiefly persons from 2 to 25 years of age. The most dangerous period, physicians agree, is from 5 to 10 years.

New Device Records Action of the Heart

SPECIAL TO THE NEW YORK TIMES | NOV. 19, 1924

SCHENECTADY, N. Y., NOV. 18. — A new machine for recording heart action, based upon the fact that the heart generates an electric current, was tested in the Ellis Hospital here tonight by heart specialists at a meeting of the Schenectady County Medical Society.

The machine was developed by the engineering laboratory of the General Electric Company at the request of physicians in this part of the country, who, many years ago, interested the late Dr. Charles T. Steinmetz in the solution of the problem of how to register the electrical impulses of what they describe as "the power house of the body."

Dr. Steinmetz's experiments were hampered by the lack of proper instruments but the development of the vacuum tube showed that it might easily be adapted to the amplification of the tiny electric impulses generated by the contraction and expansion of the heart muscles. It was with that more recent knowledge in mind that, when Louis T. Robinson, director of the engineering laboratory, was asked by physicians to produce an electrocardiograph that would be portable and accurate, he volunteered to undertake the task.

The machine exhibited to a large body of physicians and surgeons, including several heart specialists from New York and other cities, was the result of several months of effort by Mr. Robinson and H. B. Marvin, also of the laboratory. Mr. Marvin explained that the instrument measures the voltage difference between various parts of the body. It is actuated by the electrical energy which comes from the patient in the form of tiny electric impulses.

Dr. Hubert Mann of the Veterans' Hospital in New York City, one of those present tonight, has estimated that the electrical energy generated by the heart is equal to only one fifty-millionth of the energy used by an electric incandescent lamp. This energy is so small that it has to be amplified in the same way that a wave impulse is amplified by a radio receiving set. The voltage difference before and after the heart beat is approximately one-thousandth of a volt.

"The function of the electrocardiograph," said Dr. M. C. Clowe, President of the County Medical Society, "is to observe the electrical changes produced by the spread of the excitation wave from the auricles to the ventricles. From an electrocardiographic film, or tracing, extremely important facts concerning the rhythm and conductivity of the heart are ascertained. The excitation wave is an electrical phenomenon."

The new electrocardiograph is considered still in an experimental stage, and Mr. Robinson explained that he was demonstrating it to learn if any detailed changes were necessary to make the device better suited to their purposes. Dr. S. E. B. Pardee of the New York Hospital said that it seemed to fulfill every condition demanded.

Elaborate precautions against vibration are necessary in the type of cardiograph used at present, because of the delicate metal quartz filament of the string galvanometer utilized in them to record the electrical heart impulses. The new machine can be placed on any reasonably steady table in the patient's home. It was shipped recently by express from Schenectady to New York, unpacked, and found to be in condition for immediate use. The old type cardiograph could be moved only with great difficulty and it was impossible to ship it assembled.

CHAPTER 3

Advances Accelerate: 1930–1959

Statistics proved that the nation's death rate had plummeted in just thirty years with the use of new vaccines. Strides were made against typhoid, pellagra and influenza. The most exciting new development of all — penicillin — was hailed as "the most powerful germ killer ever discovered." Antibiotics such as penicillin changed the face of medicine forever. Yet the great strides made against disease also caused some to raise an alarm about the effects on the gene pool and the increasing burdens on doctors.

Nation's Death Rate Halved Since 1900; Diphtheria Cut 95%

BY THE NEW YORK TIMES | JULY 6, 1930

THE DEATH RATE of the nation has been cut in half since 1900 and in the case of some diseases, notably diphtheria, it has been reduced 95 per cent, it was announced yesterday in the revised report of the joint committee on health problems of the American Medical Association and the National Educational Association.

The report is the first revision of the joint committee's statistics since 1924 and is a summing up of the winning battle which medical science and education are waging against disease. The committee completed its task only last month, after more than a year's extended effort by the eighty authorities in health and education who compose it.

The report will form a new basis for health education in the United States, according to the committee's chairman, Dr. Thomas D. Wood of Teachers College, Columbia.

FIGHT ON DIPHTHERIA HAILED.

The reduction in the death rate of diphtheria is hailed as one of the most striking victories recorded in the report of medical progress in the past fifty years. The factors chiefly responsible for the reduction of 95 per cent in the mortality rate from this disease, according to the report, are the discovery of diphtheria antitoxin and of toxin-antitoxin, used to immunize children.

The decrease in the death rate for diphtheria is matched by that for typhoid and paratyphoid fever, the report reveals.

Despite the tremendous reduction in many diseases, however, the report reveals that the country still pays an appalling toll to sickness in money.

American taxpayers, the report estimates, pay more than $927,000,000 a year to care for sufferers from tuberculosis and heart disease and to assist those who are physically handicapped. Of this amount $800,000,000 goes to the tubercular, $90,000,000 to cardiac victims and $37,000,000 to the physically handicapped. Deaths from tuberculosis, it is estimated, cost the people of the United States more than $1,500,000,000 a year.

Since 1900, the report declares, the filtration and chemical treatment of water, the pasteurization of milk, and the control of carriers have cut the death rate for typhoid and para-typhoid from 34 persons per 100,000 to 4.9 per 100,000 in 1928.

The reduction was even more striking in military life, where formerly typhoid took a heavy toll. This the report illustrates by United States Army statistics. During the first two years of the Civil War typhoid caused 1,961 deaths among every 100,000 soldiers, whereas during the first two years of the World War only five soldiers in every 100,000 died of this type of disease.

The committee's report indicates that more than 31,000 soldiers' lives were saved because medical men were more successful in applying their knowledge for the prevention of typhoid during the first two years of our entry in the World War than in the same period of the Civil War.

The almost complete elimination of cholera, typhus and yellow fever, all of which took thousands of lives throughout this country during the last century, is also reported. This success is attributed to the careful studies of the causes and the application of proper preventive measures.

GENERAL DEATH RATE CUT.

A great reduction in the general death rate of the nation is one of the outstanding features of the report. Prior to 1900 the general death rate of the nation ranged between 20 and 30 per 1,000 of population. In 1928 the rate was 12 per thousand. As a result of these and other factors, the report indicates that twenty years have been added to the average expectancy of life in this country in the last seventy-five years. Thus, it declares, a child born in Massachusetts in 1925 was expected to live until it reached the age of 50, whereas such a child born in 1850 was expected to die at 30.

A great reduction in infant mortality was also effected in the last thirty years, the report shows. In 1900 more than sixteen babies of every 100 born died before reaching their first birthday. At present seven of each 100 born die during the first year. A better understanding of baby care has contributed to this, it is asserted.

The fight waged against tuberculosis has similarly been successful, according to the figures in the report. The death rate from consumption has decreased from 194 per 100,000 in 1900 to 79 per 100,000 in 1928. The causes of the decrease, the report says, include improved economic conditions, particularly among the industrial population, educational campaigns by tuberculosis associations and health departments, and the increased facilities for early diagnosis and hospitalization and care of the sick.

The decrease in tuberculosis mortality has been more pronounced among certain ages than others. Thus the least improvement has occurred among young people, chiefly girls and women between the ages of 15 and 24, according to the report. No explanation is offered for this.

CHILD'S LIFE HAS GREATER VALUE.

Owing to the increased expectancy of life in this country and the decrease in the prevalence of these diseases, the monetary value of newly born children's lives have greatly increased, so that a boy born in 1924 was potentially worth $1,780 more than such a child born in 1901 the report estimates. At that time he would have been worth $7,553, using his life expectancy and earning capacity as a basis for consideration. Thus the report estimates that the results of health education have saved this country more than $3,500,000,000 during the last quarter of a century.

Exclusive of ordinary illness in this country, it is estimated that there are 75,000 blind, 45,000 deaf and dumb, and well over 300,000 mental defectives in the United States at present. More than 700,000 persons in the United States are also crippled to an extent that interferes with their earning a living.

The expense of maintaining these individuals amounts to more than $100,000,000, the report says.

Dr. Wood declared that the 1924 report of the joint committee's work had been entirely revised. A number of new chapters have been added. The chapter on "The Trend of Health," prepared by the subcommittee of biological and public health experts, of which Dr. George T. Palmer, director of research of the American Child Health Association and a member of Hoover's child health committee, is one of the most important additions to the new report, Dr. Wood said.

Other revisions include a more detailed discussion of the immunization against preventable diseases, an elaboration of mouth hygiene, accident prevention, mental hygiene and the applications of psychology to health education.

Another new chapter is the one on "Measurements in Health Education."

AUTHORITIES WHO AIDED.

Among the authorities who aided in the preparation of the work are the following:

Committee of the National Educational Association:

Dr. A. K. Aldinger, director of health education for the New York City Board of Education.

Dr. Edna W. Bailey, University of California.

Dr. William Burdick, Maryland State supervisor of physical education.

Dr. Frank R. Rogers, director of health and physical education, New York State Department of Education.

Dr. John M. Dodson, Chicago, chairman committee of the American Medical Association.

Dr. Isaac Abt, Chicago.

Dr. A. J. Chesley, St. Paul.

Dr. R. W. Corwin, Pueblo, Col.

Dr. Edward Jackson, Denver.

The technical advisory committee which was appointed to aid in the revision was composed of seven subcommittees. The chairmen of these subcommittees were:

Dr. Frederick G. Bonser, Columbia, subcommittee of educators.

Dr. L. W. Childs, Cleveland, subcommittee of physicians.

Dr. Percival M. Symmonds, subcommittee of educational psychologists.

Dr. Percy R. Howe, Boston, subcommittee of dentists.

Dr. Mary S Rose, Columbia University, subcommittee of nutrition experts.

Miss Ethel Perrin, New York, subcommittee of physical educators.

Dr. George T. Palmer, subcommittee of biological and public health experts.

In addition there was a technical committee of twenty-seven appointed to aid the others in their tasks.

Virus Character Radically Changed

BY WILLIAM L. LAURENCE | JUNE 19, 1936

ROCHESTER, JUNE 18. — Transformation for the first time of the virus of one specific disease into the virus of another specific disease, hailed as a new land-mark in medical progress, was reported here today before the Summer meeting of the American Association for the Advancement of Science by Dr. George Packer Berry, Dr. John A. Lichty and Helen M. Dedrick of the Department of Bacteriology, School of Medicine and Dentistry, University of Rochester.

Viruses are micro-organisms so small that they pass through the pores of porcelain filters which hold back ordinary bacteria. It is not known whether they are living organisms, like bacteria, or twilight creatures existing in the hazy borderland between the living and the non-living.

But whatever they may be, the viruses are among the deadly enemies of man, animal and plant. In man they produce such a widely separated variety of plagues as infantile paralysis, encephalitis, yellow fever and the common cold.

Each of these diseases, and a host of other virus-produced ills, is engendered by a specific virus which causes its own specific disease and no other.

NEW RESEARCH FIELD HELD OPEN

The Rochester scientists have for the first time succeeded in changing one virus, which until now has produced in rabbits a specific disease known as rabbit fibroma, into another virus which produces an entirely different disease in rabbits, known as infectious myxomatosis.

The fibroma virus produces a benign local tumor which is harmless, whereas the virus of the second disease produces an infectious, malignant, cancer-like tumor which is fatal to the domesticated rabbit.

For purposes of illustration, this scientific achievement may be said to be the equivalent in the submicroscopic world of changing one breed of animal into another of a similar species — say a domesticated cat into a tiger.

The success of changing for the first time one virus into another is believed to open up a new field of research into the nature of all the other viruses, including those that attack man.

The possibility suggests itself that similar processes go on in nature, with less virulent viruses somehow becoming transformed, under as yet unknown conditions, into the viruses of the more virulent kind. Efforts will now be made to determine whether or not such conditions exist, and if they do, to find means for preventing them.

"We suggest," Dr. Berry stated, "that experiments similar to these may prove useful in exploring the natures of other viruses and their relationships, possibly their role in the animal pox group, in the foot and mouth disease group, and in the causation of tumors."

The latest achievement in alchemy also promises to shed new light on the composition of the viruses.

In making their first "synthetic virus," the Rochester scientists took the living specimens of the non-virulent type and mixed them with the dead "carcasses" of the virus of the virulent, cancer-producing type.

Upon injecting the mixture of the dead and living into rabbits, the living viruses are found to have taken on the nature of the dead, as though the dead had taken possession of the body of the living.

Before mixing, the virulent viruses are heated for half an hour at temperatures between 60 and 75 degrees centigrade. These temperatures have been found in repeated experiments to inactivate the virus, as their injection in rabbits produces no effect whatever.

DEAD VIRUS COMES TO LIFE

But while they are completely inactivated when acting by themselves, the report stated, the dead come to life when they are brought in contact with the living viruses of rabbit fibroma. The fibroma virus seems to "give up its own ghost" in exchange for the ghost of its dead relative.

The "ghost" has been found to be able to withstand temperatures up to 75 degrees centigrade. When boiled to a heat of 90 degrees it has been found to lose its power of resurrection through the body of the fibroma virus, Dr. Berry reported.

"Something in the myxomatous material, heat-resistant up to 75 degrees centigrade, and by itself unable to induce myxomatosis in rabbits, changes fibroma virus into myxoma virus," he stated.

These experiments support the hypothesis, he added, that fibroma virus and myxoma virus are different strains of one basic virus.

This opens the way to further hypothesis that viruses producing different diseases may be offshoots of similar basic strains, so that an inactivated virus may suddenly come to life and produce a fatal disease by making contact with a living, though relatively harmless, virus.

The "synthetic virus," like its natural prototype, the report added, has the power to propagate itself in the living body of rabbits or in culture media containing living tissue. The disease it produces has been found to be exactly the same as that produced by the natural myxoma virus.

The studies also promise to furnish new clues on the evolution of disease and on the effect of new environment on susceptibility to disease, Dr. Berry pointed out.

When the first English colonists came to America they brought with them European rabbits which they domesticated. The descendants of these rabbits are today the only variety susceptible to the myxoma virus, whereas neither their European parents, nor their relatives, the native American cotton-tail rabbits, are subject to this disease.

The reason for this difference in susceptibility, it is believed, hides secrets of the relationship of environment to the evolution of disease and to immunity to particular diseases.

TUBERCLE BACILLUS WAX DIFFERS

Progress in the chemical analysis of the wax coatings of the bacillus of tuberculosis, which seem to cover the deadly germ like a hard, impenetrable turtle shell and afford it protection against the body's armies of defense, was reported before the meeting by Dr. R. J. Anderson of the Department of Chemistry, Yale University.

Dr. Anderson recently reported the isolation, in an intensive study during the past nine years, of 170 different chemicals manufactured by the tubercle bacillus, with at least twice as many still to be found.

While the study of the wax coatings is not yet completed, Dr. Anderson said, a preliminary survey of their chemical composition "indicates quite clearly that decided differences exist between the waxes of the human tubercle bacillus and the avian and animal type of the same bacillus."

The extension of the recently developed technique for determining the blood groupings of ancient Egyptian mummies to enable similar determination of the blood groupings of the ancient fossilized skeletons of even earlier man was reported by Dr. P. B. Candela, Brooklyn physician.

Chemical Is Found to Combat Viruses

BY THE NEW YORK TIMES | FEB. 11, 1938

A CHEMICAL AGENT that has cured distemper in dogs, ferrets and cats, the first drug in medicine to cure, as well as to prevent a disease due to a virus, is announced in the current issue of Science, official organ of the American Association for the Advancement of Science.

The report is presented by Professor Alphonse R. Dochez and Dr. C. A. Slanetz, department of medicine and department of animal care, College of Physicians and Surgeons, Columbia University, and the Presbyterian Hospital. Professor Dochez is widely known for his identification of a virus as the primary agent in the common cold.

There are types of diseases due to micro-organisms. One type, such as pneumonia and tuberculosis, is caused by living organisms that are visible under the microscope. These are grouped under the general term bacteria.

The second type is caused by micro-organisms that are invisible even under the most powerful microscope and pass through the finest porcelain filters that keep bacteria from passing through. These are known as the filterable viruses and are responsible for a host of dread diseases in man and animals, including infantile paralysis, encephalitis, rabies, smallpox, measles and yellow fever.

FEW DRUGS FOR BACTERIAL ILLS

Few drugs have been found for even the diseases of bacterial origin. The best known of these are quinine for malaria, which is due to a parasite salvarsan for syphilis, and the more recent sulfanilamide, which has produced spectacular results in the treatment of diseases due to streptococci.

For the diseases caused by a virus, however, no chemical agent has so far been found to combat these invisible organisms, which recently have been found to be giant protein molecules, belonging neither to the realm of the living nor non-living, but dwelling somewhere in the mysterious borderland between the two.

The discovery by Professor Dochez and Dr. Slanetz thus holds out promise of double significance. From an immediate practical point of view the new drug has been found to prevent as well as to cure distemper in dogs and cats, thus providing a specific new remedy for a generally fatal animal disease.

Second, and of possibly even greater importance, is the promise that medical science has at last broken the ice, as it were, in finding a specific drug for preventing and curing a disease of a virus origin. This may pave the way for the development of similar drugs for the prevention and cure of human diseases caused by the various viruses.

The new chemical is known as sodium sulfanilyl sulfanilate. It contains five atoms of oxygen, three atoms of hydrogen, two atom of nitrogen, two atoms of sulphur and one atom of sodium.

A CRYSTALLINE SUBSTANCE

This compound, the report states, is a white crystalline substance highly soluble in water and of neutral reaction, adding: "It is readily absorbed by way of the gastro-intestinal tract, and has little or no toxicity for small animals in dose equivalent to one gram per kilogram of body weight. Ferrets, rabbits and cats have received one gram per day for periods as long as two weeks without loss of weight, appetite or other untoward symptoms."

The drug was first used experimentally on ferrets by producing the disease artificially. After these experiments had proved that the drug is harmless to the animal and that it serves both as a preventive and a cure, the drug was used clinically on dogs seriously ill with spontaneous distemper.

"Of twenty-eight animals treated at varying stages of the disease," the report states,

twenty-six have recovered. Symptoms and fever disappear rapidly and *the appetite promptly returns. The animals remain well after cessation of treatment.*

One animal treated on the fifth day of the disease recovered within forty-eight hours and thereafter remained well. The amount of drug administered to dogs has been one gram twice daily.

Eighteen cats suffering from a spontaneous disease commonly known as cat distemper or influenza have also been treated with the drug. Its effect in this condition is in all respects similar to that in canine distemper.

The drug therefore appears to be the first chemical agent to have such definite therapeutic action in an infection due to a filterable virus. The range of its activity in virus diseases remains to be explored?

TRIES NEW DRUG IN CANCER
Dr. Strong Reports Mice Cured of Disease of Breast

A chemical distilled from oil of wintergreen has been found to soften and in some cases completely to dissolve spontaneous cancer of the breast in mice, it is reported in the current issue of Science by Dr. Leonell C. Strong of the Department of Anatomy, Yale University School of Medicine.

The chemical is known as heptyl aldehyde, an ingredient of the fraction of the oil of wintergreen that has a low boiling point as compared with the high boiling point ingredient of the oil, namely, methyl salicylate.

"A very pronounced softening and liquefaction of the tumors occurred in the mice receiving heptyl aldehyde in an otherwise normal or standard diet," Dr. Strong reports.

Liquifaction was so extensive that drainage through a hypodermic needle under sterile conditions was easily accomplished.

Six of the first twenty-five mice placed on the heptyl aldehyde treatment completely regressed their tumors. Liquefaction and regression of tumors never occurred in 120 individuals which served as controls. Samples of the drained-off liquid were tested by Dr. C. G. Burn and found to be sterile.

Dr. Strong first observed that oil of wintergreen has an inhibitory effect on breast cancer in mice. As the high boiling point fraction of the oil produced no effect, he experimented with the fraction having a low point.

> It was demonstrated, he reports, that the low fraction had a pronounced effect on (1) the slowing up of the growth rate of tumors, with complete regression in four out of thirty-four animals; (2) an increase in the survival time of the mouse after the onset of cancer, and (3) gross and histological alterations in the tumors themselves.
>
> These changes in the tumors themselves were (1) softening, and in some cases (2) complete liquefaction. The action of the low fraction appeared to be more pronounced than the action of the true oil of wintergreen. Since heptyl aldehyde is an ingredient of the low fraction, it was decided to put mice bearing spontaneous tumors of the mammary gland on a diet containing this chemical.

It is a long way from mice to men and no conclusions can be drawn as to whether or not this chemical may prove of value in the treatment of human breast cancer, or if so, whether it would also be efficacious in other types of cancer.

However, until now no chemical had been found to have a similar effect on breast cancer in a mammal, and the discovery must therefore be regarded as another milestone in man's fight against his "natural enemy No. 2," it was pointed out.

Hails 'Blood Bank' as Transfusion Aid

SPECIAL TO THE NEW YORK TIMES | FEB. 20, 1938

PHILADELPHIA, FEB. 19. — A "blood bank," which has been in operation at the Philadelphia General Hospital less than four months, has been used in more than 400 blood-transfusion cases, with results described today as just as effective as if the blood had been drawn from a human donor instead of from a sterile wash bottle.

The technique, which stores refrigerated human blood for use in subsequent transfusions, has been so successful that Dr. William G. Turnbull, superintendent of the hospital, has received a request for information from the British Red Cross Society. He now wants a big refrigerator for "Bank No, 2."

The present "bank," according to hospital attachés, is saving taxpayers' money in reduced laboratory costs, besides saving lives.

Formerly when blood was needed for a transfusion, prospective donors had to be rounded up by telephone, police messengers or radio broadcasts and their blood had to be typed and analyzed, the practice causing a delay of several hours.

Now when a patient needs a transfusion, the "bank" of blood is waiting and the whole process is a matter of a few minutes, just long enough for a simple check of the blood in the "bank" with that of the patient.

The blood has been taken in advance from a donor and mixed with 10 per cent by volume of a solution of sodium citrate, which prevents the clotting together of the red blood corpuscles. Three more small test tubes of blood are collected at the same time. One is sealed and attached to the wash bottle in which the solution is placed. The others are sent to the laboratory, one for typing, the other for Wasserman study.

When the reports are received by the "bank," the results, with the name of the donor, the date and any information as to his having recovered from a long list of infectious diseases, are entered in a card index file under the type of the blood, 1, 2, 3 or 4.

Meanwhile the blood has been placed in the refrigerator, in a temperature maintained constantly at 39 degrees Fahrenheit. It usually can be kept in the "bank" for two weeks before hemolysis takes place, and some has been kept as long as six weeks.

When a patient needs a tranfusion the hospital informs the family that there is no charge but states that it would appreciate some blood contributions if the family knows any donors. In this way the "bank" obtains its "deposits."

"Poor people are very generous," said Dr. Charles S. Cameron, chief surgical resident.

"The response is amazing. Sometimes we get as many as a dozen or fifteen donors through one suggestion of that kind."

Vaccine Is Found for Yellow Fever

BY THE NEW YORK TIMES | MARCH 23, 1938

THE DEVELOPMENT OF a new vaccine that has proved effective against yellow fever in actual applications in South America was announced yesterday by the Rockefeller Foundation in a report by its president, Dr. Raymond B. Fosdick.

The vaccination in 1937 of more than 38,000 persons in Brazil and about 2,000 in Colombia, Dr. Fosdick said, "gives every indication that efficient protection of populations exposed to jungle yellow fever is in sight."

"Beginning in 1931," Dr. Fosdick added, "the staff of the laboratory of the International Health Division of the Rockefeller Foundation in New York was successfully vaccinated with a modified virus, the action of which was further dampened by the use of relatively large doses of human immune serum. Although effective, this method proved too cumbersome and expensive for widespread application.

"For this reason, attempts had been made during the past several years to develop more highly modified strains of virus which would require little or no immune serum."

The new vaccine, it was revealed, achieves this end, eliminating the need for immune serum, and thus making its application much less expensive.

"The reaction to this vaccine," Dr. Frederick revealed, "is mild in comparison with the after effects of immunization against other disease organisms.

"The results of the vaccination with this virus have been measured by the mouse protection test, also developed in the Foundation's New York labratory, in some 700 persons who were previously inoculated with living virus. Of these persons, over 99 per cent showed full or partial immunity."

Conquest of Pellagra

BY THE NEW YORK TIMES | JUNE 19, 1938

THE ISSUE OF State-controlled medicine so dominated the proceedings of the American Medical Association that little attention was paid generally to the scientific reports. These were of the usual varying merit, ranging, as they did, from the discussion of the effect of politics on the intestinal tract to the relation of hormones to the determination of sex. One paper that must be regarded as a milestone was that presented by Drs. Tom D. Spies, William Bennett Bean and Robert E. Stone. It left no doubt that pellagra has been conquered by means of nicotinic acid and its compounds.

As far back as 1914 Dr. Joseph Goldberger of the United States Public Health Service had concluded that pellagra was not an infectious disease. Like Walter Reed, he daringly decided to experiment on human volunteers. His subjects, Mississippi convicts, were to earn their freedom by living on such typical Southern agricultural fare as corn meal, cane syrup, hominy grits, fat salt pork. When six out of eleven were laid low, Goldberger's case was proved. Pellagra turned out to be the consequence of a deficiency of vitamin B2.

Vitamin B2 is a complex. What is the curative factor? To C. A. Elvejhem of Wisconsin and his associates goes the credit for identifying it as nicotinic acid. For the acid cures black tongue, the canine equivalent of human pellagra. A dozen brilliant clinicians took the hint and began to experiment on humans. It is hard to assign the credit for priority. Thanks to grants from the Josiah Macy and Rockefeller Foundations, Dr. Spies and his associates were able to make the most far-reaching experiments, and to prove the efficacy of nicotinic acid in 199 patients and the possibility of tiding the poor population of the South over those seasons of the year when milk, eggs, fresh meat and green vegetables are scarce.

What this success means the statistics proclaim eloquently enough. So far as the United States Public Health can determine, 400,000

Epidemiologist and United States Public Health Service member Dr. Joseph Goldberger.

people succumb to pellagra in this country every year — an underestimate. If the diet is not corrected the death rate is as high as 69 per cent. Worse still, the mind is affected. Fully 10 per cent of the inmates of our institutions for the mentally afflicted suffer from pellagra. To restore the victims to health of body and mind by adding to the proper food doses of a cheap chemical seems miraculous. The work that has been done by Dr. Spies and his associates in Birmingham, Ala., and in Cincinnati leaves no doubt that an ailment which has baffled medicine for centuries has at last been relegated to the curable diseases, and that American medicine has to its credit a triumph comparable with the conquest of yellow fever.

'Giant' Germicide Yielded by Mold

BY WILLIAM L. LAURENCE | MAY 6, 1941

ATLANTIC CITY, N. J., MAY 5 — A new chemical substance elaborated by a special strain of mold in bread and Roquefort cheese that has proved itself in tests on animals and in preliminary clinical trials on human beings as the most powerful non-toxic germ-killer so far discovered, thousands of times more potent than any of the drugs of the sulfanilamide family, was described here today.

Hundreds of leading physicians from the United States and Canada, attending the annual meeting of the American Society for Clinical Investigation, heard Dr. Martin H. Dawson, Associate Professor of Medicine at the College of Physicians and Surgeons, Columbia University, New York City, report on the new germ-killer.

Associated with Professor Dawson in this work, which physicians here hailed as opening a new chapter in the fight of medical science against bacterial infections caused by the vast host of deadly microorganisms known as gram-positive bacteria, were Drs. Gladys L. Hobby, Karl Meyer and Eleanor Chaffee.

NOT AVAILABLE IN PURE FORM

The new substance, not yet available in pure form, is known as penicillin, after the family of molds known as penicillium. Only one specific strain of it can elaborate the new giant among germ-destroyers, and its final isolation, Professor Dawson said, would depend on a larger supply of the starting material than is now available. However, even in its present crude form, Dr. Dawson reported, minute doses have proved remarkably effective in protecting animals against enormous doses of deadly bacteria of various types.

Recent experiments have shown, Professor Dawson reported, that penicillin is "extremely active" in a dilution of one to 500,000. Mice infected intraperitoneally (through injection of bacteria directly into the peritoneum) with a highly virulent strain of hemolytic (blood destroying) streptococci in amounts up to two cubic centimeters of whole culture, containing from 50,000,000 to 100,000,000 organisms, were protected with a dose of about seven milligrams of a "soluble, impure preparation," given subcutaneously. Control animal receiving the same bacteria in dilutions of one part in 10,000,000, Dr. Dawson reported, died within forty-eight hours.

"In further experiments," Dr. Dawson reported, "it has been shown that penicillin is effective intravenously and intraperitoneally as well as subcutaneously. Animals have also been treated successfully as long as eight hours after infection. Experiments on oral administration are as yet incomplete."

Penicillin, Professor Dawson reported, has been administered to four patients suffering from that deadly form of bacterial heart disease known as sub-acute bacterial endocarditis. "Sufficient material was not available for adequate therapy in these cases," he said. "However," he added, "no serious toxic effects were observed."

"It would appear," Professor Dawson concluded, "that penicillin is a chemotherapeutic agent of great potential significance. Penicillin probably represents a new class of chemotherapeutic agents which may prove as useful, or even more useful, than the sulfonamides."

It was originally observed by Fleming in 1929, Dr. Dawson told the physicians, that staphylococci failed to grow on plates in the neighborhood of a colony of penicillium mold.

NEW LIGHT ON GRAMICIDIN

Last year Dr. René J. Dubos startled the scientific world with the announcement that he had extracted from a special strain of soil bacteria a chemical substance he named gramicidin that had proved the most powerful microbe-killer until then known to man. Unfortunately, gramicidin was found to be highly toxic to animals as well as to bacteria.

At the meeting today there were presented two reports, from the Mayo Clinic, Rochester, Minn., and from the Massachusetts Memorial

Hospital, Boston, respectively, announcing studies on the gramicidin that have made it possible to apply it successfully in a number of human infections that had not responded to any other treatment.

Dr. Wallace E. Herrell and Dr. Dorothy Heilman of the Mayo Clinic, set out to determine, by methods of tissue culture the manner in which gramicidin produced its toxic effects on animals. They found that along with its powerful bactericidal action it also possessed the power to break down red blood cells by the process called hemolysis. This at once indicated that the chemical might be used safely in local infections where it was not necessary to introduce it into the blood stream.

Tests on animals proved that this was the case, and that the gramicidin could be used safely in local applications, as it did no harm at all to tissues. It has been used effectively, the Mayo and Boston physicians reported, in the treatment of sinus infections, infections of the bladder, infected but not bleeding wounds, ulcers and empyema from pneumonia.

The Boston report was presented by Drs. Charles H. Rammelkamp and Chester S. Keefer.

Sinus infections were cleared up within forty-eight hours, Drs. Herrell and Heilman reported. Severe bladder infections that the sulfa drugs did not affect were cured within one week.

Infected wounds were freed of all bacteria within twenty-four hours after gramicidin treatment, following which the wounds rapidly healed, Drs. Rammelkamp and Keefer reported.

Chemicals Excelling Sulfa Drugs as Germ Killers Are Disclosed

BY WILLIAM L. LAURENCE | SEPT. 10, 1943

PITTSBURGH, SEPT. 9 — A new group of anti-bacterial chemicals approaching in potency the germ-killing powers of that new wonder-drug, penicillin, and providing the first clues to penicillin's chemical identity, believed to hold the key to a new promised land in medicine, was described here today at the meeting of the American Chemical Society.

The isolation from the green cheese mold penicillin notatum, from which penicillin is extracted, of a second substance, named penicillin B, which is nearly ten times as potent a germ-killer as penicillin, was also discussed at the meeting. Penicillin B, isolated by a group of workers at St. Louis University, kills bacteria in dilutions as high as 1,000,000,000 to 1 (billion to one). Unfortunately, it is even more rare than the original penicillin, on the extraction of which America's major chemical houses are now concentrating, with the cooperation of Government agencies. The entire output is reserved for the armed forces.

The new germ-killing chemicals belong to a chemical group known as acridines, composed of three benzene rings joined together and containing one atom of nitrogen in each ring. The nitrogen atom at the lower end of the center ring gives this group a characteristic color.

AIDING WOUNDED IN AFRICA

One member of the acridine group, proflavine powder, has already been used with great effect on wounded soldiers in North Africa by two British physicians, Drs. G. A. G. Mitchell and G. A. H. Buttle, who use it in the healing of battle wounds that did not respond to sulfa drugs, it was reported.

The bacteria-destroying powers of some of the acridines, it was reported, are as much as a hundred times those of the sulfa drugs. New members of the family recently synthesized, it was stated, are active in dilutions of 10,000,000 parts to one. Penicillin A, in some instances, acts in dilutions of 160,000,000 to one.

Studies revealing for the first time how these new penicillin-like chemicals produce their effects on germs, opening the way to the synthesis of a host of related chemicals even more potent than those now in existence, were described by Dr. Gustav J. Martin of the Warner Institute for Therapeutic Research, New York City.

The great Paul Ehrlich sought for the "magic bullet" which would destroy bacteria directly without harming the patient, but such direct-acting "magic bullets" are almost impossible to find. The discovery of the sulfa drugs provided a new approach to chemotherapy.

BACTERIA ARE SURROUNDED

These drugs do not act as "magic bullets" by destroying bacteria directly. Instead, they act indirectly by surrounding the bacteria with a "chemical magic wall" as it were, which makes it impossible for the bacteria to obtain a food substance vital for their growth. Thus weakened through lack of food, the bacteria fail to multiply. The body's infantry, the white blood cells, then steps in and wipes out the isolated remnants.

The acridines, Dr. Martin found, also exert their effect in an indirect way, but instead of building a chemical wall around the bacteria that deprives them of an essential food factor, the acridines, Dr. Martin found, put the germs in a "chemical vacuum" in which they are deprived of oxygen, the staff of life for most bacteria as it is for other living things. Whereas the sulfa drugs produce starvation, the acridines cause asphyxiation.

The human body as well as bacteria utilize oxygen by means of vital enzyme systems, known as respiratory enzymes, which make possible chemical union between cells and the oxygen from air, water and from food substances. An important group of oxygen-carrying enzymes contains the chemical constellations known as adenines. It is these adenine-containing enzyme systems, Dr. Martin found, that are

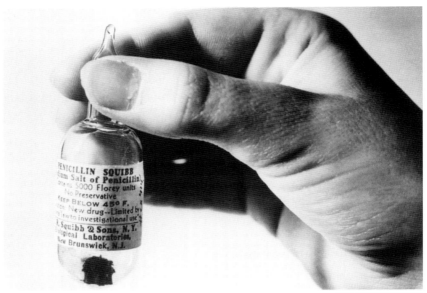

An ampoule of penicillin. The finished product is a greenish brown powder. It takes about 500 quarts of culture fluid to make one ounce of penicillin.

interfered with by the acridines, and without these adenine enzymes the bacteria are literally suffocated.

Just as too little oxygen is bad for bacteria and man, too much oxygen is equally bad, causing the body's energy fuels to burn too fast, hence, an excess of oxygen-carrying enzymes is also harmful to bacteria, Dr. Martin pointed out.

Penicillin B, the chemical constitution of which has been found by the chemists at St. Louis University to contain an important oxygen-carrying group, acts in exactly the opposite manner from that of the acridines. Instead of depriving bacteria of oxygen, it surrounds them with too much oxygen, in the form of hydrogen peroxide. This results in literally "burning" the bacteria alive.

Thus these new studies of the acridines provide two highly important strategic highways for storming the citadel of disease-producing bacteria. One is to synthesize new members of the acridine family, more potent than those now in existence, to deprive the bacteria of vital oxygen. The other would be to create substances that would produce the same effect as pencillin B, namely, super-carriers of oxygen.

The observation on the manner in which pencillin B produces its death-dealing effect on bacteria, Dr. Martin said, may shed light on the nature of the chemical action of the first member of the family, now known as pencillin A.

When the organism produces two different chemicals, it is often the case that the two act as opposites, one counterbalancing the other. Because of this it may be reasoned that pencillin A and pencillin B are also two parts of what may be called a "gyroscope of life."

THE A MAY INHIBIT THE B

Since penicillin B acts as super-carrier of oxygen, it was pointed out, it is not unreasonable to assume that penicillin A acts as an inhibitor to penicillin B, preventing it from supplying too much oxygen. If that is the case, Dr. Martin stated, then penicillin A may produce its effect in the same manner as the acridines, and may even turn out to be a member of the acridine group.

There was excitement here today when the rumor spread among the chemists that penicillin A has already been sythesized by a large pharmaceutical house. No confirmation could be obtained of the report, which, if true, would be one of the greatest milestones in man's age-old struggle against disease, of vast importance to our armed forces and civilians alike.

If such a synthesis has actually been achieved, it was pointed out, it may very likely be kept a military secret for the time being, at least, or until means are available for quantity production of this wonder-chemical, to satisfy civilian as well as military needs.

New Drug Is Used to Treat Typhoid

BY THE NEW YORK TIMES | MAY 24, 1945

STREPTOMYCIN, THE GERM-KILLING qualities of which were revealed only a year ago, has been used successfully in the treatment of typhoid fever, a disease for which to date there has been no known positive cure, it is disclosed in the current issue of The Journal of the American Medical Association.

Of five persons treated who had been infected with typhoid through a germ carrier reportedly stemming from a bakery, three were completely cured, and in the two other cases the authors suggested that certain human body substances were present that inhibited the influence of the streptomycin.

These new experiments with streptomycin, which indicate its effectiveness in combating Gram-negative bacteria, against which penicillin has been used without success, were conducted last December by three Philadelphians. Their studies are the first publicly reported successful experiments in treating typhoid with streptomycin.

The scientists are Dr. Hobart A. Reimann of the Jefferson Medical College and Hospital, who directed the clinical studies, assisted by Dr. Alison H. Price of the same institution and Dr. William F. Elias of the Wyeth Institute of Applied Biochemistry, who handled the laboratory tests.

While purely in the experimental stage, streptomycin was nevertheless said to present the first good approach to a cure for typhoid, which scientists have sought for ages, but thus far they have developed only a conservative fever treatment.

The experiments also indicated a probable superiority of streptomycin, originally discovered by Dr. Selman A. Waksman of Rutgers University, over penicillin in the long-range treatment of such diseases as tuberculosis. With few exceptions, penicillin has proved of little value in the treatment of these diseases.

In the Philadelphia experiments, the five individuals were treated over a period of one to two weeks each and received daily dosages of streptomycin.

The patients were treated with streptomycin orally as well as intravenously and intramuscularly with success, although the oral treatment alone was ineffective. The report suggested, however, that oral treatment with streptomycin in typhoid areas might prove useful in preventing the disease in the same manner that atabrine is successful in preventing malaria.

Streptomycin is available in limited quantities and is provided for experimental uses only. It was described by one scientist not connected with the Philadelphia experiments as in approximately the same stage of development for general public use as penicillin was two years ago.

Streptomycin has been used successfully in the treatment of tuberculosis in guinea pigs in experiments at the Mayo Clinic by Drs. W. H. Feldman and H. C. Hinshaw, but results of the treatment of tuberculous patients with streptomycin have not yet been reported publicly.

Influenza Vaccine Perfected in War

BY THE NEW YORK TIMES | MARCH 9, 1946

ANTI-INFLUENZA VACCINES perfected as the result of wartime research have freed mankind from the scourge of uncontrollable influenza epidemics, Dr. Wendell M. Stanley of the Rockefeller Institute for Medical Research, Princeton, N. J., said last night after the presentation to him of the William H. Nichols Medal of the American Chemical Society's New York Section. The medal, one of the highest honors in chemistry, was presented at a dinner in the Hotel Pennsylvania.

Dr. Stanley, who was cited for "his outstanding contributions to the chemistry of the virus," said that the vaccines, now being made for civilian use, had "placed in our hands the means for preventing influenza virus from once again assuming the role of one of the great destroyers of human life." The methods evolved for producing the vaccines are such, he added, that even if some unknown strain of influenza virus should appear, protection against it could be developed in a matter of days.

It was the fear that a repetition of the influenza pandemic of 1918 might cripple America's war effort that led to intensive study of the disease at the outset of the last war. The 1918 pandemic, Dr. Stanley explained, was one of the three greatest outbreaks of disease within the knowledge of man; afflicting an estimated 500,000,000 persons throughout the world and taking 15,000,000 lives.

"At the height of that pandemic," he said, "people were dying at the rate of one out of every fifty persons in the world a month, a death rate unsurpassed in history. In the United States alone 500,000 persons died in four months."

Thus the destruction of human life by influenza within a four-month period was greater than our losses during the years of this greatest of all wars, he asserted.

No means of protection against a major outbreak of influenza was available in 1941, he added, and "with the advent of war, the mixing of populations and the accompanying strains and stresses, the possibility of a major influenza epidemic loomed as a dreaded spectre."

Presentation of the medal was made by Dr. Ralph H. Mueller of the Radiation Laboratory of the Massachusetts Institute of Technology, who is chairman of the jury of award. Speakers included Prof. Vincent du Vigneaud, head of the biochemistry department, Cornell University Medical College, and Dr. Ralph L. Shriner, chairman of the Department of Chemistry, Indiana University, Bloomington. Dr. Cornelia T. Snell, chairman of the New York Section, presided.

Doctors Describe a Heart Reviver

BY WILLIAM L. LAURENCE | OCT. 24, 1950

BOSTON, OCT. 23 — An electrical pacemaker that has been used success-fully in animal experiments to make hearts that have stopped beat again was described here today before the opening sessions of the annual clinical congress of the American College of Surgeons.

The new technique and apparatus were described by Drs. J. C. Cal-laghan and W. G. Bigelow of the Department of Surgery, University of Toronto, Canada. They stated that the procedure was "safe in animals, allows complete control of heart action and successfully maintains blood pressure."

It has been possible, they added, "to take over control of heart action, in hearts beating at normal or at reduced rates, by impulses from an electrical artificial pacemaker, and to increase or decrease the heart rate at will."

When developed further, the new pacemaker is expected to find use-ful application in cases of serious cardiac arrest, for a period long enough to enable the heart to resume functioning. It also offers promise, in cases of irregular heartbeats, to restore the heart's action to normal rhythm.

Drs. Callaghan and Bigelow also expressed the hope that their Pace-maker might lead to the direct surgery on the heart as well as to the restoration of normal heart action following exposure to extreme cold.

The pacemaker consists of electrodes that are inserted through an incision in the region of the natural pacemaker of the heart. The elec-trodes are then supplied with an electrical stimulus by means of a thy-ratron physiological stimulator capable of delivering single impulses that can be controlled easily.

TWO MEANS OF CONTROL

Two means of delivering impulses are used. One consists of single impulses under foot-pedal control, the other of automatic impulses, delivered at a desired rate and regulated by a frequency-control dial.

It had been observed before, the doctors stated, that "complete standstill of the heart occurred quite frequently at very low body temperatures. It was also noted that application of a stimulus, whether electrical or mechanical in character, to the region of the sinoauricular node resulted in the production of normally appearing expulsive beats.

"An attempt was therefore made to develop a technique whereby frequent regular electrical stimuli of required strength and character could be applied to the sinoauricular nodal area to act as an artificial pacemaker, which might permit control of heart action for prolonged periods after cardiac arrest."

Cardiac arrest which occurs at low body temperature (hypothermia), they reported, has proven suitable for study of the artificial pacemaker, "and control of cardiac function has been affected."

"We have proposed the use of general hypothermia as a means of reducing the oxygen requirements of the body sufficiently to allow exclusion of the heart from the circulation and thus permit intracardiac surgery under direct vision," they asserted. "The use of an artificial pacemaker will allow a resuscitation should cardiac arrest occur during the procedure."

REPORTS ON ARTIFICIAL HEARTS

Reports on the development of improved artificial hearts, to take over circulation of the blood and thus make possible direct surgery upon damaged hearts, were presented by investigators from a number of laboratories.

The reports came from Investigators at the Tufts College Medical School and New England Center Hospital; Mount Zion Hospital of San Francisco, Yale University School of Medicine, the Montefiore Hospital, New York City; the Graduate School of Aeronautical Engineering, Cornell University, and the University of Toronto Faculty of Medicine.

However, none of these artificial hearts is as yet ready for application to human beings, and many problems will have to be solved before this can be done.

Dr. Charles A. Hufnagel of the Harvard Medical School and the Peter Bent Brigham Hospital described a method, tried so far only on dogs, for directly widening the outlet tract of the right heart. The technique employs a preserved arterial segment to increase the cross sectional area without interruption of the already existing flow.

"This procedure," Dr. Hufnagel stated, "is suggested particularly for the treatment of stenosis (stricture) of the outlet tract below the pulmonary valve, but it is also effective at all levels."

Dr. Frederick A. Coller of Ann Arbor, Mich., in his address as retiring president tonight, stated that the special bill to draft doctors, recently passed by Congress, "was an unwarranted denial of our past performance and was carried through in an atmosphere of confusion and lack of understanding of us that we have come to expect."

Dr. Coller expressed the hope that a "medical audit" of hospital efficiency would be adopted by all hospitals. "It is as iniquitous," he said, "to condone and shield from scrutiny the poor work of an incompetent colleague as it is to pursue our own methods of therapy regardless of end results. The medical audit gives a fair test of competency and can be made a yardstick of skill and achievement, and should serve as an educational method of surpassing value."

He warned against "certain members of our profession who assume that the right conferred upon them by the states to practice medicine and surgery carries also the right to carry out any surgical procedure that they may wish to attempt, regardless of their skills."

Fanfare Ushers Verdict on Tests

SPECIAL TO THE NEW YORK TIMES | APRIL 13, 1955

ANN ARBOR, MICH., APRIL 12 — The formal verdict on the Salk vaccine was disclosed today amid fanfare and drama far more typical of a Hollywood première than a medical meeting.

The event that made medical history took place in one of the University of Michigan's most glamorous structures — Rackham Building. Television cameras and radio microphones were set up outside the huge lecture hall. Inside the salmon-colored hall a battery of sixteen television and newsreel cameras were lined up across a long wooden platform especially built at the rear.

At 10:20 A. M. Dr. Thomas Francis Jr., director of the Poliomyelitis Vaccine Evaluation Center and the man of the hour, was introduced. A short, chunky man with a close-cropped mustache, he was wearing a black suit, white shirt and striped gray tie.

He stepped behind a lectern decorated with a blue and gold banner bearing the seal of the university. He appeared small, hidden up to his breast pocket by the lectern, as he looked out toward his audience of 500 scientists and physicians. Cameras ground and spotlights played upon him. Then Dr. Francis adjusted his horn-rimmed glasses and began to read his long-awaited report in a slow, conversational tone. It was the report of a meticulous and dedicated scientist, presented without dramatics.

Nevertheless, the moment was a dramatic one, no matter how hard the Professor of Epidemiology tried to make it otherwise with his charts and statistics and careful qualifications. The nation and the world had been waiting for this report, a report that could mean hope for millions of parents and a great step forward in the control of paralytic polio.

Dr. Francis talked for an hour and forty minutes. Occasionally he would step back from the lectern. The lights would dim out and a slide would be flashed on a screen behind the lectern. Dr. Francis would

Dr. Jonas Salk displaying the polio vaccine that he developed in a University of Pittsburgh laboratory.

call attention to various statistics and chart illustrations by pointing a flashlight on the screen.

The audience was quiet and respectful. There were no bursts of applause. Even at the end of Dr. Francis' address, after he had made it clear that the Salk vaccine had been proved an effective weapon, the applause seemed restrained.

Outside the hall, however, the Hollywood atmosphere prevailed. Students and the curious crowded close behind television cameras set up for interviews with medical celebrities. In a press room three floors above, more than 150 newspaper, radio and television reporters were sending out details.

Actually word of the findings had been sent out before Dr. Francis began to talk. University public-relations officials brought 300 copies of the report to the pressroom at 9:15 A. M.

Although there had been purported leaks regarding the report, university officials had denied they were authentic and had put up a well-nigh impenetrable barrier around the evaluation center.

It was disclosed today that Dr. Francis did not finish writing his report until 3 A. M. last Friday. It was not until late Thursday evening, according to Robert B. Voight, statistician for the center, that Dr. Francis and his staff reached the point where they could set down accurate estimates.

There was other evidence of the tight security. Dr. Jonas E. Salk, who developed the vaccine, acknowledged that he had not had an opportunity to read the report. Basil O'Connor, president of the National Foundation for Infantile Paralysis, indicated that he had not seen it in advance either.

With Dr. Salk today in his hour of triumph were his wife, Mrs. Donna Salk, and three sons, Peter, 11 years old; Darrell, 8, and Jonathan, 5. The two older boys were among the first to be inoculated with the vaccine developed by their father.

Much attention was focused throughout the day on Dr. Salk, who had spend long hours in the laboratory to make this day possible.

Mrs. Salk seemed somewhat embarrassed by all the attention. She said that she and her family would be glad when things calmed down again and they could return to normal life.

Biochemist Fears Rise of the Unfit

RICHARD J. H. JOHNSTON | MAY 20, 1958

OMAHA, NEB., MAY 19 — Interference through medical progress with the processes of natural selection in humans "may be a step toward racial suicide," a research biochemist said today.

Dr. Rene J. Du Bos of the Rockefeller Institute for Medical Research voiced the warning at the annual convention of the National Congress of Parents and Teachers.

Although bigger and apparently stronger children are being raised, he said, discoveries in preventive medicine do not necessarily make them more fit to survive.

"For the first time in the history of living things," he continued, "we are allowing the survival of large numbers of biological misfits, many of whom will become a burden for society. Even more significant is the fact that all kinds of hereditary defects that used to be rapidly eliminated by evolutionary selection are now being reproduced in our communities."

REFERS TO DEFECTIVE GENES

Through the application of medical knowledge in treating diseases, he warned, "we are allowing the accumulation of defective genes in the human stock by providing a type of medical care that permits those suffering from hereditary disease to live longer and to have children.

"While the preservation of human life is demanded by moral, social and religious considerations, we are now engaged in a process which may result in ultimate dangers," he cautioned.

"This policy may constitute a step toward racial suicide, however noble it may appear in the light of our religious convictions and present-day ethics."

Dr. Du Bos said he did not advocate "a retreat from our human ideals and medical ethics." However, he went on, "we must and will continue to regard all life as sacred and worth preserving whatever the cost."

"We also must be aware of the consequences of the new demands and values that we have introduced into the biological arena," he said.

The problems of disease in society "cannot be solved merely by discovering new drugs or inventing new surgical techniques," he commented. A reevaluation of social ethics is needed because of the "inevitable limitation of resources" that must be imposed on decisions of the future, he said.

EDUCATION SPEED-UP URGED

Another speaker in a symposium on "the changing social scene in America" was Dr. David H. Dawson, vice president, of E. I. du Pont de Nemours & Co.

He called for speeding up the educational system to produce the highest degrees of talent while fitting the less talented for the skilled jobs that the automated future would offer.

He urged more competition among students in the class-room to prepare them for competition in adult life.

Eric Johnson, chairman of the Committee for Economic Growth, spoke at the general meeting tonight. He pleaded for support of President Eisenhower's foreign aid program.

Known Viruses Now Exceed 300

BY NORTH AMERICAN NEWSPAPER ALLIANCE | DEC. 7, 1958

WASHINGTON, D.C. — Eighty viruses infesting humans have been discovered in the last ten years.

These are in addition to previously known agents of such maladies as smallpox, yellow fever, measles, mumps, forms of influenza and a host of other infectious maladies. The number of viruses now known, both plant and animal, exceeds 300.

The effects of most of the newly discovered "semi-organisms," which have many attributes of life although they cannot be described as alive, remain unknown. Some may be harmless, others may be responsible for unknown or hitherto misdiagnosed diseases.

Scientists of the Public Health Service's National Institute of Health have made major discoveries, including groups of viruses responsible for types of colds, especially in children.

Most of the new agents are too small to be seen with the ordinary microscope. What they look like has been known only since the perfection of the electron microscope. Most of those affecting man appear to be spherical. Those found in plants are elongated particles.

The largest, which causes psittacosis, or parrot fever, has a diameter of 1/83,000th of an inch, the smallest 1/2,500,000th. This range bridges the gap between the size of protein molecules and bacteria.

Viruses have been objects of mystery since their discovery forty years ago. However, a health service bulletin says, "The sum of definitive information about them is now growing rapidly."

"Viruses have been called 'living chemicals,' " the bulletin notes.

It is evident that they have important attributes of living things — ability to achieve reproduction, variation and selective survival.

But the virus cannot survive and multiply away from other living matter. They impel the cell to supply the chemicals they need for reproduction, even at the expense of the cell's own life and function. This

parasitism may be latent and symptomless, or explosive and destructive.
A yellow fever infection, for instance, may represent a massive attack on
body cells. It has been estimated that a thousand million virus particles
may be produced during an attack.

The body's defense system normally responds with remarkable speed.
Antibodies against the invader are manufactured that adhere to the
molecules or micro-organisms against which they are developed. Once
activated, the defenses often remain for months, years or a lifetime. Anti-
bodies may be stimulated by vaccines. They are ready to go into immedi-
ate action if a virulent form of the microbe is encountered.

Some new-found members of the family are very dangerous. Such, for example, is the "salivary gland virus" studied at the institute. In at least 10 per cent of healthy nursery-age children in cities, it is found to be dormant, but in some cases it causes destructive degenerative disease in various organs. Generalized infection may cause death.

It also is known to attack the central nervous system in early infancy, or before birth, resulting in mental deficiency.

Doctor's Dilemma: How to Keep Up

BY LEONARD ENGEL | JUNE 7, 1959

DURING THE PAST two decades, every year has brought a bumper crop of advances in medicine, many of lifesaving importance. One result has been a pressing new problem for the practicing physician: how to keep up-to-date.

The lives of the doctor's patients depend on his possession of the latest medical knowledge. But it is hard for the busy physician to find time to keep up with even a part of the ever-increasing discoveries in medical science.

"Many doctors do a good job of staying abreast of major new developments," says a medical school dean, "and give their patients thoroughly modern care. Unfortunately, this isn't true of all. Many have little real opportunity to keep up. Some don't even try."

In recent months, medical leaders have been discussing numerous schemes for altering this situation. The most drastic proposal has come from Dr. Gunnar Gunderson, president of the American Medical Association. Dr. Gunderson has said that, if other measures fail, he wants compulsory periodic licensing examinations for all physicians — perhaps every five years.

The doctor's task in keeping up-to-date is not only urgent, but formidably complex.

"The physician must keep up in a double sense," says Dr. Norton S. Brown, president of the New York County Medical Society and a member of a New York Academy of Medicine committee studying the problem. "During his training, the doctor was schooled to high standards of medical workmanship. He was taught to study each patient with painstaking care. He owes it to his patients to maintain these standards despite the pressures of a crowded waiting room and an endless round of hospital and house calls.

"Somehow, he must also find time to keep pace with what's new.

New drugs, for example, come out at a dizzying rate — several hundred a year. The physician has to know something of most or all of them — even the many that are no real improvement over existing drugs. And he must learn a great deal about those that are truly new and useful — a task that can easily consume a man's full time. Yet new drugs constitute only a small part of medical advance."

No doctor, of course, can familiarize himself with the details of new developments in all areas of medicine. This is one reason why two of every five physicians in active practice in the United States choose to be specialists. But even the specialist must know at least the broad outlines of what is being accomplished in branches of medicine other than his own.

"That's the part that keeps me reading nights and week-ends," says one New York practitioner. "I couldn't do a decent job for my patients otherwise."

A few weeks ago, a symposium on heart surgery was held at Mount Sinai Hospital in New York as part of a postgraduate course sponsored by the American College of Physicians. The speakers were six cardiac surgeons with world reputations. The audience was composed entirely of internists — specialists in internal ailments who perform no surgery. I asked an internist from Texas and another from Ohio why they were there.

"To find out which of our patients the heart surgeons can help," they replied.

Internists and general practitioners must be equally well posted in many other areas of medicine. They see most patients before other physicians. They need to know about advances in psychiatry, for example, since they may see patients in the early stages of mental illness. Moreover, psychological factors figure prominently in a number of the ailments — such as peptic ulcer — which the internist and the G. P. treat.

It works the other way, too. Psychiatrists must be alert to advances in internal medicine and even in surgery. Thus, anti-clotting drugs and blood-vessel surgery have recently been shown to be of value in many cases of stroke. The psychiatrist may see some of these cases, for patients with incipient stroke often have vague symptoms and are sometimes sent to psychiatrists as "neurotic."

And so it goes for every branch of medicine, from allergy to radiology. There is no branch that cannot profit from advances in another.

How does the practicing physician keep up with changes in medicine today?

Let us see how one doctor who does a conscientious job of keeping up goes about it. Dr. A. — the code of medical ethics forbids use of the name of a doctor in private practice — was graduated from medical school twenty years ago and is now in his mid-forties. His office is in a big city suburb and he has a general family practice.

One afternoon and one evening each week he drives fifteen miles to the city to serve in a diagnostic clinic in a large hospital with a strong teaching program. His motive is not the nominal fee he receives ($13 per session), but contact with a teaching hospital.

Rank-and-file doctors and medical educators alike agree that the most effective device by far for keeping a doctor's standards high and his knowledge fresh is contact with a teaching hospital. Unfortunately, only several hundred of the 7,000 hospitals in the United States (chiefly medical-school hospitals) have effective medical teaching programs.

Dr. A. finds three aspects of his clinic work valuable. One is the wide range of patients he encounters. Another is the opportunity to work with an alert group of residents (young doctors taking specialty training) and with specialists. The third is the informal contact afforded him with members of the hospital staff.

"I don't know which aspect of the clinic work is most helpful," Dr. A. declares. "The clinic is a constant reminder of how medicine ought to be practiced. Since this is a teaching clinic, every hospital resource is used to obtain all relevant data on each patient. Every patient is studied as a demonstration case.

"But I especially enjoy the opportunity the clinic work gives me for talking with other doctors at the hospital. This is a pretty lively hospital. Something new is always being tried. I hear about it in consultations over difficult cases, in the corridors, in the doctors' lounge, or when I go to dinner with some of the staff."

Dr. A. also goes to meetings at the hospital to hear discussions of medical journals. In addition, he goes on ward rounds every few weeks, usually when he hears of interesting patients.

Although the city hospital is the focus for Dr. A.'s "keeping up" activities, he does not leave it at that. Once or twice a month, he attends medical society lectures. Each year, he goes to a medical convention or takes a one- or two-week post-graduate course. And he subscribes to nearly a dozen medical journals, which he generally gets to look at in bed after midnight.

"Sometimes I wonder whether I ought to cut down on the journals and get a little more sleep," Dr. A. remarks. "But then something happens that makes me pleased as punch that I do stay up and read.

> The other week, a patient came to me with a complaint of ringing in the ears, dizziness and nausea — a combination of symptoms called Meniere's disease, ordinarily caused by disease of the auditory nerve. I was about to send him to an ear-nose-throat man for ear surgery — the usual treatment for Meniere's disease — when I recalled an article I had read a few weeks before in a British medical journal. An English physician had eleven patients in which Meniere's syndrome turned out to be due to an ulcer or other ailment of the digestive tract rather than to disease of the auditory nerve.
>
> I sent my patient for gastrointestinal X-rays. Maybe it was pure coincidence. But there wasn't anything wrong with his auditory nerve. He had a gastric ulcer, possibly cancerous.

The majority of physicians do not have Dr. A's opportunity to participate in the activities of a first-class teaching hospital. However, the practicing doctor who wants to practice up-to-date medicine has a rich assortment of other educational aids to choose from.

On a volume basis, the most important is the vast array of medical journals available to him. In the United States alone, well over 1,000 journals devoted to medicine as a whole or to its various branches are published. The total is higher still if journals in fields related to medicine, such as physiology, are counted.

In fact, finding journals that can inform him of new developments is not the doctor's problem. The hard part is choosing which journals to read. A medical editor recently pointed out that if a surgeon were to devote every evening in the month to reading only the principal journals of general surgery in the English language — all containing much information not duplicated in other journals — he could not get through one month's issues before the next crop descended upon him.

This flood of reading matter has given rise to a host of other publications, designed to single out and summarize the most significant reports published in medical journals or given at medical meetings. These include review and abstract (digest) journals, books, monographs and pamphlets, and special bulletins issued by agencies such as the American Heart Association. In addition, pharmaceutical companies put out magazines and newspapers — many well-edited and widely read — for physicians.

Doctors may also buy digests of medical reports recorded on tape, to be played while driving about on house calls. And closed-circuit TV has been utilized both to bring information on new developments like the Salk vaccine to nation-wide medical audiences, and to demonstrate new surgical procedures at medical conventions.

But the educational activity considered most useful by physicians — especially physicians with little opportunity to work in teaching hospitals — is the post-graduate "refresher course." More than 2,000 of these are offered each year by medical schools and organizations like the American College of Surgeons. They generally last one to two weeks and they cover an immense variety of subjects.

In 1955 the American Medical Association questioned 4,923 of 168,000 practicing physicians in the United States on what they did to keep up with new developments in medicine. The survey showed that many put in an impressive amount of time reading, attending lectures and refresher courses and holding discussions with other doctors. Conscientious specialists reported spending 750 hours (equivalent to nearly ninety-five eight-hour days) a year in such activities; general practitioners reported almost 550 hours a year.

But the survey also disclosed two weaknesses in the various programs devoted to helping the doctor keep up. For one thing, many of these activities were found to be of limited value. Thus, numerous physicians found medical society lectures much less effective than journal reading; and journal reading was described as not to be compared either with attendance at post-graduate courses or with work in a teaching hospital.

The second weakness disclosed by the A. M. A. study is the fact that 30 per cent or more of practicing physicians take little or no part in medical society programs or other formal educational activities. What information they have on new medical developments comes chiefly from occasional journal reading or from "detail men" — the pharmaceutical company salesmen who call on doctors.

"I do not mean to denigrate the detail man," says a prominent medical educator. "The detail man deserves much of the credit for the speed with which new drugs are brought into wide use today.

However, the detail man comes to the doctor's office to sell drugs. Aside from the fact that drugs constitute a very small part of medicine, the detail man sees the physician for a few minutes only. In that time, he can pass on only the sketchiest sort of data on one or two drugs — data often so presented as to gloss over the limitations of the drug.

I think the detail man, and pharmaceutical over-promotion in general, share some of the blame for drug abuses. But I think the physician who depends solely on the detail man also deserves blame. That is not the way to practice good medicine.

Medical leaders agree that some sort of external stimulus is necessary to make some physicians work harder at raising their standards and at keeping their medical knowledge fresh. But they also concede that the fault does not lie entirely with the physician.

Numerous studies have shown that more "keeping up" facilities of every kind are needed, from additional teaching hospitals to post-graduate courses better geared to the requirements of the contemporary practicing doctor. The size of the need, however, is itself a sign of medical progress. If medicine were not changing so rapidly, there would be no concern over whether doctors were keeping up.

LEONARD ENGEL, as a freelance writer who specializes in medical and scientific subjects, also finds "keeping up" a major concern.

CHAPTER 4

New Diseases and New Fixes for Old Ones: 1960–1999

While vaccines continued to be developed for old diseases like mumps and measles, a new, frightening disease first showed its lethal power in the gay community. Conception took place in test tubes, via in vitro fertilization, and through the first cloned creature. Cardiology took a great step forward during the first heart transplant, and through the use of new procedures to open up clogged arteries. The next generation of X-rays revealed even more of the human body.

Vaccines Hailed as Measles Doom

BY HAROLD M. SCHMECK JR. | FEB. 11, 1965

THERE IS NO LONGER any excuse for the 4,000,000 or more cases of measles that develop yearly among American children, a specialist said here yesterday.

The comment was made by Dr. Saul Krugman of New York University School of Medicine during a news conference called to announce the licensing of a new live virus measles vaccine. The vaccine was put on the market yesterday by the Pitman-Moore Division of the Dow Chemical Company, Indianapolis, after authorization by the National Institutes of Health.

The news conference was held at the New York Academy of Sciences, 2 East 63d Street.

The first live virus measles vaccine was marketed in March 1963, by Merck & Co. Late last year two others also became available, one marketed by Eli Lilly & Co. and the other by Philips Roxane, Inc., a subsidiary of Philips Electronics & Pharmaceuticals, Inc.

SEVERAL AVAILABLE

With several effective vaccines available, Dr. Krugman said at the news conference yesterday, "there really is no longer any excuse for any child in this country to have to endure this disease."

Dr. Krugman and other speakers noted that the complications of measles could be serious and, sometimes, even fatal.

Dr. John J. Witte, an epidemiologist of the United States Public Health Service's Communicable Disease Center in Atlanta, said it was estimated that there were four million or more cases of measles yearly in the United States. He said that a significant reduction could not be expected until there was a wide use of vaccine against measles.

Dr. Witte said 450 to 500 deaths a year were directly attributable to complications that develop from measles cases. Some of these deaths are caused by encephalitis — inflammation of tissues of the brain — and others by pneumonia that follows the measles attack.

BRAIN DAMAGE

In about one out of every 1,000 cases of measles there is some residual brain damage, the available statistics indicate.

Dr. Morton Andelman of the Chicago Department of Health said measles was a more formidable public health problem in terms of the disability it causes, than poliomyelitis ever was.

The new vaccine, marketed under the trade name Lirugen, is given in one injection that is believed to offer long-term, probably lifetime, immunity. Wholesale price a dose will be $2, a spokesman said. It has not been found necessary to give gamma globulin with the new vaccine to diminish the frequency of such undesirable side effects as fever or rash. Gamma globulin is often given with the other live virus measles vaccines.

Dr. Krugman, who has done epidemiological studies with the new vaccine, said it gave extremely prompt protection. The incubation period of the virus used in it is shorter than that of the "wild" measles virus, he said.

Therefore a child given the vaccination any time before, or even shortly after, exposure to measles will probably be protected.

A Mumps Vaccine Is Licensed by U.S.

BY HAROLD M. SCHMECK JR. | JAN. 5, 1968

WASHINGTON, JAN. 4 — The Government has licensed the nation's first live virus vaccine against mumps, a disease believed to strike about 80 per cent of Americans before adulthood.

The United States Public Health Service recommends the vaccine primarily for children approaching puberty, for adolescents and adults, especially males, if they have not had mumps.

The peak season for mumps is late winter and early spring. Most cases occur in children between the ages of 5 and 15, but the most serious cases are likely to occur in adult and adolescent males.

Among these as many as 25 per cent may have infections that spread to the reproductive organs, with possible adverse effects on fertility. Documented cases of sterility caused by mumps are considered rare, however.

The vaccine will not be recommended for routine use in younger children until more information becomes available on the duration of its protective effects.

A license for the vaccine was granted to Merck, Sharp & Dohme, of West Point, Pa., after an 18-month study of its safety and potency by the Division of Biologic Standards of the National Institutes of Health.

The pharmaceutical company, which developed the vaccine during the last five years, said nationwide distribution of one million doses would begin Monday.

In youngsters, the disease involves a painful, extensive swelling of the salivary glands in the throat. Serious complications in young children are unusual.

The big question concerning the vaccine is how long it will give protection against the disease. Only if it proves able to give long-term immunity could it be recommended for widespread use in children.

Such immunity cannot be conclusively proved until persons who have already received it have been followed for several years.

Among 6,500 susceptible children and adults who were given the vaccine, 95 per cent developed protective antibodies against mumps, the Public Health Service advisory committee on immunization practices said.

The committee said the vaccine should not be given to children under a year of age because they may have anti-bodies from their mothers that would interfere with the vaccine's effect.

In a live virus vaccine, the virulence of the virus has been markedly weakened.

The vaccine should not be given to anyone who is ill with any fever-producing disease.

On theoretical grounds, the committee said, vaccination against mumps should probably be avoided in women who are pregnant.

The new live virus vaccine should not be given to anyone allergic to eggs, chickens, or to the antibiotic neomycin.

The vaccine was developed primarily by Dr. Maurice R. Hilleman and Dr. Eugene B. Buynak of Merck's research laboratories.

The company said field trials of the vaccine, involving more than 16,000 persons, had been carried out by 25 teams of doctors in 43 studies. The original virus strain was isolated from Dr. Hilleman's daughter, Jeryl Lynn.

Body's Rejection of Heart Feared

BY HAROLD M. SCHMECK JR. | DEC. 4, 1967

WASHINGTON, DEC. 3 — The heart transplantation reported from South Africa is an event many medical scientists have been expecting in recent months although none could say when, where or by whom such an attempt would first be made.

Years of experimentation with animals here and abroad laid the groundwork for this attempt.

In some of the animal research cases, dogs have lived more than a year with transplanted hearts. In related studies, animal hearts have been stored in cold saline solutions for as long as seven hours and then successfully transplanted and restarted in other animals.

American scientists who pioneered in this research say the surgical problems of heart transplantation have largely been solved.

The key question that still remains is insuring that the recipient's body will not react against, and destroy, the foreign heart.

Even after a surgically successful transplant such as the one in South Africa, the question of preventing this immunological rejection process must hang over the case for days, weeks and possibly for months or years.

In almost all transplantation, whether it be of the heart or another organ, the main issue is preventing this native tendency for a living body to destroy transplanted foreign tissue.

To minimize the danger of this rejection process the surgeons try to choose as donor and recipient in any transplant case two people as closely alike, genetically, as possible. That is why the surgeons in South Africa were careful to match the blood type of the heart patient and his donor.

But blood typing is not sufficient to guarantee success. Complex tissue typing methods are used in the United States in kidney transplantation where the greatest experience has been gained.

Even these tissue typing methods, however, are considered far from perfect.

As a further defense against immunological rejection, drugs are ordinarily given to the transplant patient. The mainstay is usually a drug called Imuran, a compound chemically related to certain anti-cancer drugs.

Steroid hormone preparations such as prednisone are also given in many cases. Regular treatment with Imuran is usually continued indefinitely after the transplantation. The steroid is usually given only when a rejection crisis seems imminent.

One new preparation, called anti-lymphocyte globulin, is also viewed as a highly promising agent to prevent rejection.

From the standpoint of surgery alone, the South African case is neither the first attempt to save a human life by heart transplantation nor the first attempt to transplant a human heart.

On Jan 23, 1964, the heart from a healthy chimpanzee was transplanted into a man dying of chronic heart disease.

The attempt was made by Dr. James D. Hardy of the University of Mississippi Medical Center, Jackson, Miss. The patient's heart stopped beating before the transplant attempt was made. His circulation was supported in the interim by a heart-lung machine.

The chimpanzee heart beat strongly for an hour and a half, then stopped and could not be restarted. The patient died. The surgeon concluded that the animal heart had been unequal to the task of maintaining the circulation of a man.

Surgeons at the Medical College of Virginia recently transplanted a heart into a baboon from a human being killed in an accident. The purpose was to see whether such a salvaged heart could be revived to work again. In this case the heart did restart but soon failed.

Dr. Richard P. Lower, who described the experiment earlier this fall to the American College of Surgeons, said he believed that the cause was a powerful immunological rejection response in which the baboon's body had rejected and destroyed the human heart as a functioning organ.

At the same meeting, however, Dr. Lower showed a film clip of a dog running and wagging its tail. The heart that kept the dog alive was transplanted from another dog more than a year earlier.

The surgeon said that two dogs had lived as long as 15 months with transplanted hearts and that the transplanted hearts functioned well.

The Journal of the American Medical Association recently quoted Dr. Norman E. Shumway of the Stanford Medical Center of Palo Alto, Calif., as having said that surgeons were on the threshold of trying heart transplantation in human patients.

"We think the way is clear for trial of human heart transplantation," said Dr. Shumway, pioneer in this research.

Dr. Shumway told the medical journal that the first attempt in man would require that an ideal donor and an ideal recipient be available at the same time.

Choosing the appropriate recipient is difficult because no doctor would think of removing a patient's heart for such a highly experimental attempt until it was clear that the patient's own heart had deteriorated beyond useful recall.

But that means that the patient must be at the brink of death before the transplantation attempt will be made.

The ideal donor, Dr. Shumway said, is a relatively young man or woman who died of causes basically unrelated to the heart. He said experimental evidence had shown that if the heart could be removed from the donor within a half-hour after death it could be resuscitated without suffering damage.

The crucial need is to get the heart cooled substantially below normal temperature as soon as possible. The California surgeon's research has shown that animal hearts can be kept in cold storage as long as seven hours and still be restarted.

To date surgeons at several institutions here and abroad have tried to transplant the human liver, lung, kidney and now the heart, as well as other tissues and organs less vital to life.

The kidney remains the only vital organ with which really long-term success has been achieved.

Even with the kidney transplantation experience that now totals more than 1,000 cases over a span of more than 13 years, failures are common and more research is believed needed.

In contrast, even if the South African case does succeed, human heart transplantation remains only at the threshhold of surgical experience.

X-Ray of Entire Body Shows Color TV Image

BY STACY V. JONES | NOV. 29, 1975

WASHINGTON, NOV. 28 — A professor at Georgetown University Medical School here was granted a patent this week for his X-ray machine, which can scan the whole body, or any organ, and immediately show a color picture on a television screen. In effect, it makes a bloodless incision, displaying in cross-section any part of the body.

The machine, for which Dr. Robert S. Ledley was awarded Patent 3,922,552, is being manufactured in Silver Spring, Md., by a subsidiary of Pfizer, Inc. More than 50 of the machines have been sold to hospitals, and half of these are already installed. The current price is $340,000.

Dr. Ledley believes he developed the first whole-body computerized tomographic scanner. In tomography, a cross-section of the body is pictured.

The patient is passed through the machine on a stretcher. A framework carrying on one side a source of X-rays and on the other a receiver rotates about the body. The computer digests the information for display in a single plane. Two pictures of adjacent areas are made simultaneously.

A common use for the machine is to precisely locate and determine the size and shape of a brain tumor. If the physician knows the approximate location, he can place a marking on the patient's head. The patient can be placed for scanning any part of the body, such as kidneys or pancreas. The scanning assembly can be tilted for the best possible picture. According to the patent, the machine can scan any portion of the body with equal efficiency and accuracy. Other advantages are said to be a high degree of adjustability and reduced radiation doses.

The inventor is professor of physiology, biophysics and radiology at the medical school. A physicist, he also holds a degree in dentistry.

New Procedure Aids Some Heart Patients

BY RONALD SULLIVAN | JUNE 17, 1978

A NEW MEDICAL PROCEDURE that opens clogged coronary arteries by inflating a tiny, catheter-induced balloon inside of them has been developed by Lenox Hill Hospital for some patients as a relatively safe and less costly alternative to highly expensive and often risky coronary bypass surgery.

Dr. Michael S. Bruno, the director of the hospital's department of medicine, said that "selected patients who otherwise would need heart surgery could undergo this procedure with little risk and at one-tenth the cost of coronary bypass surgery."

The procedure involves snaking a catheter, inserted into an arm or leg artery, through the opening of a coronary artery and then into the smaller arteries that feed blood to the heart muscle.

When the tip of the catheter reaches the spot where the artery is blocked, a tiny balloon is inflated. The inflated balloon presses the soft plaque or fatty tissue that is blocking the artery flat against the artery's interior wall, thus allowing blood to move freely and restoring normal pressure on either side of the blockage.

RESULTS 'MOST FAVORABLE'

Thus far, 31 patients have undergone the procedure, 10 of them in the catheterizatior laboratory of Lenox Hill Hospital. All 10 patients were fully awake during the procedure, and Dr. Simon H. Stertzer, the cardiologist who performed the procedure, said that the results "have been most favorable."

He said that subsequent findings showed no buildup of the blockage that had been pressed into the artery wall and that there was, instead, evidence of "a healing process."

Dr. Stertzer said he was convinced that the new technique had "tremendous potential" as an alternative to coronary bypass surgery, a complicated and sometimes risky procedure in which a blocked section of a coronary artery is bypassed with a grafted section of a blood vessel taken from the patient's leg.

Dr. Bruno told a news conference at the hospital on Thursday that the new technique could be used in 10 to 15 percent of the 70,000 patients who underwent coronary bypass surgery last year. He estimated the savings in the "hundreds of millions of dollars."

NARROWER SERVICE IS DEVELOPED

Dr. Stertzer said that seven of the 10 patients at Lenox Hill underwent the procedure successfully, and that the three others had to have bypass surgery because the catheters could not reach the obstructions.

He said the key to using the catheter instead of bypass surgery was the successful development of a narrower, more flexible device that could go beyond the point where the coronary artery branches into smaller arteries that lead to the heart's muscle.

Consequently, he said, coronary catheterization, heretofore strictly a diagnostic procedure, to determine the extent of coronary disease, could now be employed as a therapeutic procedure.

Both Dr. Bruno and Dr. Stertzer emphasized that the procedure was limited to treating coronary blockages that were composed of soft tissue, and that bypass surgery most likely would still be required for blockages involving plaque that had calcified.

Both physicians and Dr. Eugene Wallsh, chief of cardiovascular surgery at Lenox Hill, said that the new procedure had "tremendous potential" at a time when the high cost and limited therapeutic results of bypass surgery were coming under increasing criticism.

They also agreed that they would have preferred to have waited longer before announcing the procedure, so as to have long-term evaluations of the patients to present. But they said that there was "so much competition" from other hospitals and "so much interest" in the new procedure that they had agreed to make their results public even though they conceded that their conclusions may be "premature."

Dr. W. Gerald Austen, chief of surgery at Massachusetts General Hospital in Boston, said he was aware of the procedure, but he was somewhat skeptical of the therapeutic claims made by Lenox Hill.

"They have very little data and not much follow-through information, so it's too early to draw any conclusions," Dr. Austen said. But he added that the catheterization technique "was a very interesting approach that deserves careful monitoring."

With that in mind, Dr. Austen said that the new technique would be used on an experimental basis at Massachusetts General, in cooperation with Dr. Stertzer.

According to Dr. Stertzer, the balloon catheter was invented by Dr. Andreas Grunzig, a cardiologist at University Hospital in Zurich. He said that he and Dr. Richard Myler of San Francisco were working with Dr. Grunzig in perfecting the technique and in organizing its introduction into the treatment of coronary disease in this country.

Woman Gives Birth to Baby Conceived Outside the Body

SPECIAL TO THE NEW YORK TIMES | JULY 26, 1978

LONDON, WEDNESDAY, JULY 26 — The first authenticated birth of a baby conceived in laboratory glassware and then placed in the uterus of an otherwise infertile mother occurred last night, apparently without complications.

Reports from Oldham General and District Hospital in Lancashire said the baby, a girl, was delivered by Caesarian section, appeared normal and weighed 5 pounds 12 ounces.

The birth culminated more a than dozen years of research and experimentation by Dr. Patrick C. Steptoe, a gynecologist, and Dr. Robert G. Edwards, Cambridge University specialist in reproductive physiology.

UNABLE TO CONCEIVE

The parents are Mrs. Lesley Brown, 31 years old, and her husband, John, 38, a railway truck driver from Bristol.

Mrs. Brown in more than 10 years of marriage had been unable to conceive a child because of a defect in the oviducts, or Fallopian tubes, which each month carry egg cells from the ovaries to the uterus. It is during this passage that the egg cells are fertilized.

In the procedure that culminated in last night's birth, an egg cell was removed surgically from Mrs. Brown's ovaries last Nov. 10 and fertilized with sperm from her husband in a petri dish. After two or more days in a laboratory culture, the fertilized embryo was injected into Mrs. Brown's uterus.

More conventional methods had been attempted in an effort to get Mrs. Brown to conceive, including surgical reconstruction attempted in an effort to get Mrs. Brown to conceive, including surgical reconstruction of her oviducts. But the efforts failed, and about two years ago she turned to Dr. Steptoe and Dr. Edwards for treatment.

There have been previous reports of so-called "test-tube babies" but none have been authenticated. The Steptoe-Edwards efforts, which failed a number of times, have been followed closely by the medical profession.

While the experimenters have often been frowned upon, they also are highly regarded by many in the field of obstetrics.

Working with a succession of patients, Dr. Edwards has gradually improved his ability to manipulate the hormones that control the reproductive cycle.

PERFECTION OF TECHNIQUE

Dr. Steptoe has used a surgical procedure known as laparoscopy to enter a woman's abdomen at the appropriate moment in her monthly cycle to retrieve one or more egg cells. The device, placed through a small incision near the navel, illuminates the target area and allows the surgeon to identify and withdraw by suction nearly mature egg cells.

Once the egg cells have been exposed to sperm, and once microscopic examination after a few days has shown that an embryo is developing normally, the embryo is placed in the uterus with a tube inserted through the cervix.

It is estimated that one-fifth to one-half of women who are sterile are unable to bear children because of absent, defective or blocked oviducts. Because of that, it can be assumed that there will be considerable pressure on physicians to repeat the performance of Drs. Steptoe and Edwards, even though their work is still at a very experimental stage.

The chief problem encountered by the two doctors has been obtaining a satisfactory implant of the embryo in the wall of the uterus.

PROBLEMS WITH HORMONES

In normal reproduction, the embryo lingers a day or more in the oviducts after fertilization and does not implant itself until, through cellular division, it has reached a multicelled stage.

This process is controlled by hormones issued from various organs, including the ovaries, and from the embryo itself. The early efforts of Drs. Steptoe and Edwards were frustrated because their performing part of this process outside the body upset the hormonal signalling system.

Furthermore, the woman in many of the attempts was given added hormones to induce multiple egg production. The doctors hoped that this would give them more egg cells, improving their chances of success, but the added hormones seemed to throw the normal reproductive system off-balance.

Another fear was that culturing the embryo in glassware for four and a half days, as had been done, might place too severe a strain on it.

EXPERIMENTS ON MONKEYS

Shortly before their removal of one or more egg cells from Mrs. Brown last Nov. 10, it was learned from experiments at the University of Birmingham Medical School that rhesus monkey-embryos inserted into the uterus after only one or two cell divisions could survive.

This suggested that the embryos of primates, including man, might differ from other mammals in being able to withstand implantation into the uterus at so early a stage.

Some specialists therefore suspect that Drs. Steptoe and Edwards may have decided to implant Mrs. Brown's embryo after only two days, allowing it to enter the uterus well before its normal implantation stage.

Reports from the hospital this morning said that the baby was born just before midnight and that its condition was "excellent." Mrs. Brown and her husband were reported to be jubilant.

Once the fetus began developing, its own hormonal signals generated all the effects of a normal pregnancy. Mrs. Brown is reported to have experienced the sort of cravings often reported by pregnant women — in this case, a yearning for mints.

Pregnancy Lab Reports a Success

BY WALTER SULLIVAN | MAY 12, 1981

FOR THE FIRST TIME an American woman has become pregnant following the insertion into her womb of an embryo that had been fertilized in a glass dish by sperm from her husband, it was announced yesterday in Norfolk, Va.

Several pregnancies, using a similar method and leading to normal births, had previously been achieved in Britain and Australia as well as in one unconfirmed case in India.

After a year of efforts at a clinic associated with Eastern Virginia Medical School, Dr. Howard Jones, director of the clinic, told a press conference yesterday of his first success.

He declined to identify the prospective parents or say how far the pregnancy had progressed. He said that after a fertilization clinic in France had achieved a pregnancy, the prospective mother was so beset by attention from the news organizations that she miscarried.

The first American pregnancy by "in vitro" ("in glass") fertilization comes at a time when proposed Federal anti-abortion legislation could make aspects of the procedure illegal.

The fertilization clinic of Eastern Virginia Medical School was established on March 1, 1980, after certification by Virginia's Commissioner of Health and hearings at which the project was vehemently opposed by anti-abortion forces. Vernon Jones, spokesman for the clinic, said yesterday that the certification was unrelated to the merits of in vitro fertilization.

Opposition to the procedure arises chiefly from the need, before newly fertilized eggs are inserted into the womb, of discarding those that appear abnormal. But supporters of the procedure argue that this mimics the natural process that aborts defective embryos before they are implanted in the uterus.

Laboratory fertilization is designed to cope with a kind of sterility, occurring in about one out of 500 women, in which the tubes that carry the egg cells from the ovary to the uterus are defective. Normally fertilization occurs during this journey.

By the time the fertilized egg reaches the uterus, or womb, it has begun to subdivide in the earliest stages of embryo development. It then attaches itself in the womb for gestation.

The woman made pregnant at the Norfolk clinic had lost both her tubes "because of tubal ectopic pregnancies," according to Dr. Jones. In such pregnancies the embryo becomes implanted in the tube instead of the uterus and must be removed surgically, destroying the tube.

In the laboratory procedure an effort is made to determine as precisely as possible when the mother's egg cell is ready to erupt from the ovary. A device called a laparoscope is then inserted through a small incision into the abdomen.

In the laparoscope, bundles of glass fibers carry light into the abdominal cavity while other fibers enable the surgeon to look in, seek out the ripe egg cell and extract it with a suction needle. In the Norfolk method two incisions are made, one for the laparascope and one for the needle.

It was perfection of the technique by Dr. Patrick Steptoe that, on July 25, 1978, led to the birth in Britain of Louise Brown, the first child conceived in this manner.

Once the egg is removed it is placed in a dish with a special mixture of fluids and exposed to sperm "capacitated" by chemical treatment. It was the mastery of these steps by Dr. Robert Edwards of Cambridge University that also made success possible.

After the fertilized egg has subdivided a few times in its dish, paralleling the development that occurs during descent to the uterus, the embryo is inserted into the mother's womb via the cervix in the hope that it will attach itself and develop normally.

New Homosexual Disorder Worries Health Officials

BY LAWRENCE K. ALTMAN | MAY 11, 1982

A SERIOUS DISORDER of the immune system that has been known to doctors for less than a year — a disorder that appears to affect primarily male homosexuals — has now afflicted at least 335 people, of whom it has killed 136, officials of the Centers for Disease Control in Atlanta said yesterday. Federal health officials are concerned that tens of thousands more homosexual men may be silently affected and therefore vulnerable to potentially grave ailments.

Moreover, this immune-system breakdown, which has been implicated in a rare type of cancer, called Kaposi's sarcoma, and seems to invite in its wake a wide variety of serious infections and other disorders, has developed among some heterosexual women and bisexual and heterosexual men.

At a recent Congressional hearing, Dr. Bruce A. Chabner of the National Cancer Institute said that the growing problem was now "of concern to all Americans."

The cause of the disorder is unknown. Researchers call it A.I.D., for acquired immunodeficiency disease, or GRID, for gay-related immunodeficiency. It has been reported in 20 states and seven countries. But the overwhelming majority of cases have been in New York City (158), elsewhere in New York State (10), New Jersey (14) and California (71).

Thirteen of those affected have been heterosexual women. Some male victims are believed to have been heterosexual, and to have been chiefly users of heroin and other drugs by injection into their veins. But most cases have occurred among homosexual men, in particular those who have had numerous sexual partners, often anonymous partners whose identity remains unknown.

According to both the Centers for Disease Control and the National Cancer Institute in Bethesda, Md., GRID has reached epidemic proportions and the current totals probably represent "just the tip of the iceberg." Preliminary results of immunological tests have led some Federal health officials to fear that tens of thousands of homosexual men may have the acquired immune dysfunction and be at risk for developing complications such as Kaposi's cancer, infections and other disorders at some future date.

GRID is "a matter of urgent public health and scientific importance," Dr. James W. Curran, a Federal epidemiologist who coordinates the Centers for Disease Control's task force on Kaposi's sarcoma and opportunistic infections, told the Congressional hearing. Opportunistic infections are those that rarely cause illness except in those whose immunological resistance has been lowered by drugs or disease.

More than human suffering is involved. Hospital costs have reached more than $64,000 per patient, and Dr. Curran said that if such costs are typical, "the first 300 cases account for an estimated $18 million in hospital expenses alone."

Experts currently think of GRID as a sort of immunological time bomb. Once it develops, it may stay silent for an unknown period, and then, at a later date, go on to produce Kaposi's sarcoma, an opportunistic infection, a so-called auto-immune disorder, or any combination of these.

Further, no one is certain that the immune disorder can be reversed. Many patients have survived a bout of pneumonia or other illness, only to succumb to another or to go on to develop Kaposi's sarcoma or some other fatal cancer.

'NATURAL' IMMUNITY SUPPRESSOR

GRID resembles the failures of the immunological system that complicate the treatment of many chronic disorders with steroid and other drugs that suppress the immune system. The same problem occurs among recipients of transplanted kidneys and other organs who take the immunosuppressive drugs to help prevent rejection of the organ. With immunity suppressed, the body becomes vulnerable to a variety of problems, chiefly infections by organisms that otherwise rarely cause disease.

GRID, however, is the first naturally occurring outbreak of immune suppression to affect a community of free-living people, in contrast, for example, to an epidemic in a hospital. The degree of immunological suppression is extraordinary, far greater than usually observed in patients treated with immunosuppressive drugs, according to articles in medical journals and interviews with experts.

Those experts are now reporting finding a wider range of disorders than were associated with GRID when it first came to public attention last summer. These include eye damage, lupus, I.T.P. (idiopathic thrombocytopenic purpura), certain types of anemia, and other cancers, including Burkitt's lymphoma and cancers of the tongue and anus.

Doctors are also seeing many cases of a generalized lymph gland swelling throughout the body, together with weight loss, fever and thrush, a fungal infection often found in the mouth and throat.

So far, epidemiologists have found no evidence that the condition is spread from person to person like influenza or measles. Therefore, they say, the general public need not fear an epidemic.

MANY CAUSES ARE LIKELY

Rather, Dr. Arthur S. Levine of the National Cancer Institute said, development of the syndrome seems to result from an accumulation of risk factors. Most experts say that if there is an infectious cause, it is not a single organism, but an organism acting together with another factor or factors, perhaps a drug.

Epidemiologists from the Centers for Disease Control have done studies among homosexual men with and without the immune disorder but matched in age, background and other characteristics. After testing for more than 130 potential risk factors, they found that the median number of lifetime male sexual partners for affected homosexual men was 1,160, compared to 524 for male homosexual men who did not have the syndrome. The study also found more use of sexual stimulants and illicit drugs among the GRID patients.

As further evidence against simple contagious spread, epidemiologists note that the syndrome has not spread to other family members, hospital workers or researchers on the disease.

Kaposi's sarcoma was first described in 1872 in Rumania. Until recently, it was rare in the United States, occurring chiefly in older people, usually of Italian or Jewish ancestry, and among patients receiving immunosuppressive therapy. It affected men much more commonly than women by about 15 to one. It usually developed slowly.

In recent decades, however, Kaposi's sarcoma has been found common in Africa, mainly among young people. In equatorial Africa, it accounts for 9 percent of all cancers, and in some areas it is 100 times more prevalent than in the United States. The cancer has not been linked to homosexuals in Africa, and the reasons for its high frequency there are unknown.

In its new form in this country, the course of Kaposi's sarcoma generally has been rapid and fatal. Only about 15 percent of patients treated with a combination of anticancer drugs experience any remission, as compared to the 90 percent complete response in Africa, according to Dr. Levine.

However, it is not just the cancer that is killing GRID patients. Many such patients develop infections with an often fatal parasitic illness called Pneumocystis carinii. Hitherto, that disease has been seen mainly as a complication of treatment of patients with leukemia and other cancers because their immune systems were depressed by chemotherapy.

Others succumb to cytomegalovirus infection or to a fungal infection called toxoplasmosis. By using sophisticated molecular biology tests in which the genetic messages of the various strains can be compared, scientists have found no evidence that the epidemic is due to a deadly new mutant strain.

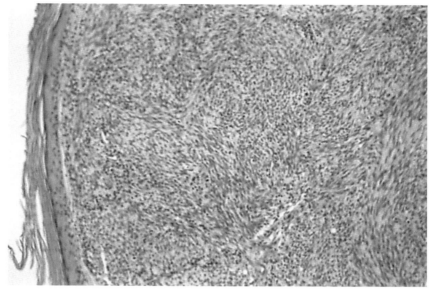

This photomicrograph of a skin biopsy shows cytoarchitectural changes of Kaposi's sarcoma.

But the list of infections diagnosed among GRID patients is long, and some of the organisms are so unusual that even the most experienced infectious disease experts have not treated a case in the past. The newest is cryptosporidiosis, a parasitic infection much more familiar to veterinarians than to physicians because it infects deer and other mammals.

WHY NOW AND NOT BEFORE?

Given the fact that homosexuality is not new, the most puzzling question is why the outbreak is occurring now, and not sometime in the past.

Scientific investigations are wide ranging, although most are focused on viruses, other organisms, drugs, or a combination of such factors.

Because homosexuals affected by GRID have reported using nitrite drugs more frequently than homosexuals who have not, some studies have focused on this class of drugs, which have come into widespread street use since the 1960's.

But although epidemiological studies have not "totally exonerated nitrites, the scientific evidence to implicate them is quite shaky," according to Dr. Curran.

Some experts theorize that the immunological disorder may be triggered by the introduction of sperm or seminal fluid into the blood through sexual contact, though infection and drug reaction are still also candidates.

In studies on mice at the National Cancer Institute, Dr. Ursula Hurtenbach and Dr. Gene M. Shearer have reported that a single injection of mouse sperm into the veins of male mice produced a profound and long-lasting suppression of certain immune functions.

Dr. Lawrence D. Mass, a New York City physician, said that "gay people whose life style consists of anonymous sexual encounters are going to have to do some serious rethinking."

The urgent need to discover the cause of the immune system disorder and to prevent the problems it creates has been underscored by Dr. Linda Laubenstein of New York University Medical Center. Dr. Laubenstein, who said she has treated 62 such patients in the last year and who is a leading investigator of the syndrome, summarized it by saying: "This problem certainly is not going away."

A Likely AIDS Cause, But Still No Cure

BY PHILIP M. BOFFEY | APRIL 29, 1984

WASHINGTON — The good news last week was that scientists at the National Cancer Institute here and at the Pasteur Institute in Paris had found viruses they believe to be the cause of AIDS, or acquired immune deficiency syndrome, a terrifying disease that destroys the body's immune system and renders its victims helpless against infections. The discovery offered hope that screening tests and, eventually, therapies will be developed to cope with the disorder. AIDS has afflicted more than 4,000 Americans, most of them homosexuals, killing about 1,750.

It was the most significant advance yet made in the fight against AIDS. It was also the signal for the scientists and institutions tracking the disease to grapple for a share of the spotlight.

Before the latest findings from the National Cancer Institute could be published in a journal and announced at a press conference, the news trickled out. First came a flurry of items emphasizing the accomplishments of Dr. Robert C. Gallo and his colleagues at the Cancer Institute and associated laboratories, who had identified and mass-produced a virus known as HTLV-3, which they consider the likely cause of AIDS. These news stories were based largely on information leaked by scientists close to the research.

Then came a flurry of articles shifting attention to a virus called LAV, which had been discovered by French scientists at the Pasteur Institute a year earlier but had attracted little interest in this country. These articles were based on interviews with key figures at institutions that were competing with Dr. Gallo to find the cause of AIDS, including Pasteur, the National Institute of Allergy and Infectious Diseases, and the Centers for Disease Control, whose researchers had worked with the French and were close to confirming the French findings.

Next came the press conference at which Margaret M. Heckler, the Secretary of Health and Human Services, left no doubt as to where she thought the credit should go. Her department had been sharply criticized for failing to move rapidly against AIDS. On Monday, she proudly announced that "the arrow of funds, medical personnel, research and experimentation, which the Department of Health and Human Services and its allies around the world have aimed and fired at the disease, has hit the target." Mrs. Heckler acknowledged the seminal work of foreign scientists almost as an afterthought. She singled out the Pasteur Institute, which had "previously identified" a virus that, she said, "will prove to be the same" as that identified by Dr. Gallo.

DIVIDE AND CONQUER

The Federal program, which Mrs. Heckler said was mobilized "without a day of procrastination," but which was accelerated at the insistence of Congress, has spent $75 million. Another $54 million has been budgeted by the Reagan Administration for the next fiscal year.

The bulk of the money has gone to the National Institutes of Health in Bethesda, Md., where Dr. Gallo has laboratories and the institute's own scientists are studying the disease. Lesser amounts have gone to the Centers for Disease Control, which are keeping track of all cases and conducting laboratory studies to identify the cause of AIDS, and to the Food and Drug Administration, which is dealing with the transmission of AIDS through blood and blood products.

By week's end, officials of all the agencies, here and abroad, were playing down the competition and blaming the press, in part, for playing it up. The history of AIDS research looks like this:

Dr. Gallo is unquestionably the pioneer in identifying and studying the family of viruses central to AIDS; indeed, his laboratory trained several members of the French team. His initial discovery was HTLV-1, which appears to cause leukemia in humans. It is widely accepted as the first human cancer virus ever identified.

Last May, in papers published in the journal Science, Dr. Gallo and his co-workers broadened their inquiry by suggesting that the same virus might also cause AIDS. At the same time, the French team singled out a variant of the virus, which they named LAV. The French buttressed their claim in a recent issue of The Lancet, a British medical journal. Now, the Gallo researchers have tacitly acknowledged that their original theory was off target, concluding instead that the real cause of AIDS is yet another virus variant called HTLV-3 — the one Mrs. Heckler said is probably identical to LAV. If it is, the French can claim credit for identifying the cause of AIDS first. "What's been lost in all this," said Walter Dowdle, director of center for infectious diseases at the Centers for Disease Control, "is that Gallo deserves tremendous credit for developing a cell line that makes it possible to grow these viruses" — that is, to mass-produce them, generating ample amounts for study. What has also been lost is the fact that the French have not had access to the cell line, which has slowed their work. Dr. Gallo's research was hailed as "a turning point in the struggle with this epidemic," by Dr. Jerome E. Groopman, an AIDS expert at New England Deaconess Hospital in Boston. But some scientists felt that Mrs. Heckler had raised false hopes by proclaiming "the triumph of science over a dreaded disease." Much more work is needed to verify that HTLV-3 or LAV is the cause of AIDS rather than an infection that often invades the weakened bodies of AIDS victims.

Federal scientists said the new finds mean that a test to detect the AIDS virus in blood supplies should be ready in six months. Some are predicting that a vaccine to prevent AIDS will be produced within two years. Others side with Dr. Anthony S. Fauci of the National Institute of Allergy and Infectious Diseases, who told reporters at a recent medical convention in Atlanta: "To be perfectly honest, we don't have any idea how long it's going to take to develop a vaccine, if indeed we will be able to develop a vaccine."

Scientist Reports First Cloning Ever of Adult Mammal

BY GINA KOLATA | FEB. 23, 1997

IN A FEAT that may be the one bit of genetic engineering that has been anticipated and dreaded more than any other, researchers in Britain are reporting that they have cloned an adult mammal for the first time.

The group, led by Dr. Ian Wilmut, a 52-year-old embryologist at the Roslin Institute in Edinburgh, created a lamb using DNA from an adult sheep. The achievement shocked leading researchers who had said it could not be done. The researchers had assumed that the DNA of adult cells would not act like the DNA formed when a sperm's genes first mingle with those of an egg.

In theory, researchers said, such techniques could be used to take a cell from an adult human and use the DNA to create a genetically identical human — a time-delayed twin. That prospect raises the thorniest of ethical and philosophical questions.

Dr. Wilmut's experiment was simple, in retrospect. He took a mammary cell from an adult sheep and prepared its DNA so it would be accepted by an egg from another sheep. He then removed the egg's own DNA, replacing it with the DNA from the adult sheep by fusing the egg with the adult cell. The fused cells, carrying the adult DNA, began to grow and divide, just like a perfectly normal fertilized egg, to form an embryo.

Dr. Wilmut implanted the embryo into another ewe; in July, the ewe gave birth to a lamb, named Dolly. Though Dolly seems perfectly normal, DNA tests show that she is the clone of the adult ewe that supplied her DNA.

"What this will mostly be used for is to produce more health care products," Dr. Wilmut told the Press Association of Britain early today, the Reuters news agency reported.

Dolly, the first genetically copied sheep, is unveiled to the media at the Roslin Institute near Edinburgh.

"It will enable us to study genetic diseases for which there is presently no cure and track down the mechanisms that are involved. The next step is to use the cells in culture in the lab and target genetic changes into that culture."

Simple though it may be, the experiment, to be reported this coming Thursday in the British journal Nature, has startled biologists and ethicists. Dr. Wilmut said in a telephone interview last week that he planned to breed Dolly next fall to determine whether she was fertile. Dr. Wilmut said he was interested in the technique primarily as a tool in animal husbandry, but other scientists said it had opened doors to the unsettling prospect that humans could be cloned as well.

Dr. Lee Silver, a biology professor at Princeton University, said last week that the announcement had come just in time for him to revise his forthcoming book so the first chapter will no longer state that such cloning is impossible.

"It's unbelievable," Dr. Silver said. "It basically means that there are no limits. It means all of science fiction is true. They said it could never be done and now here it is, done before the year 2000."

Dr. Neal First, a professor of reproductive biology and animal biotechnology at the University of Wisconsin, who has been trying to clone cattle, said the ability to clone dairy cattle could have a bigger impact on the industry than the introduction of artificial insemination in the 1950's, a procedure that revolutionized dairy farming. Cloning could be used to make multiple copies of animals that are especially good at producing meat or milk or wool.

Although researchers have created genetically identical animals by dividing embryos very early in their development, Dr. Silver said, no one had cloned an animal from an adult until now. Earlier experiments, with frogs, have become a stock story in high school biology, but the experiments never produced cloned adult frogs. The frogs developed only to the tadpole stage before dying.

It was even worse with mammals. Researchers could swap DNA from one fertilized egg to another, but they could go no further. "They couldn't even put nuclei from late-stage mouse embryos into early mouse embryos," Dr. Silver said. The embryos failed to develop and died.

As a result, the researchers concluded that as cells developed, the proteins coating the DNA somehow masked all the important genes for embryo development. A skin cell may have all the genetic information that was present in the fertilized egg that produced the organism, for example, but almost all that information is pasted over. Now all the skin cell can do is be a skin cell.

Researchers could not even hope to strip off the proteins from an adult cell's DNA and replace them with proteins from an embryo's DNA. The DNA would shatter if anyone tried to strip it bare, Dr. Silver said.

Last year, Dr. Wilmut showed that he could clone DNA from sheep embryo cells, but even that was not taken as proof that the animal itself could be cloned. It could just be that the embryo cells had DNA that was unusually conducive to cloning, many thought.

Dr. Wilmut, however, hit on a clever strategy. He did not bother with the proteins that coat DNA, and instead focused on getting the DNA from an adult cell into a stage in its normal cycle of replication where it could take up residence in an egg.

DNA in growing cells goes through what is known as the cell cycle: it prepares itself to divide, then replicates itself and splits in two as the cell itself divides. The problem with earlier cloning attempts, Dr. Wilmut said, was that the DNA from the donor had been out of synchrony with that of the recipient cell. The solution, he discovered, was, in effect, to put the DNA from the adult cell to sleep, making it quiescent by depriving the adult cell of nutrients. When he then fused it with an egg cell from another sheep — after removing the egg cell's DNA — the donor DNA took over as though it belonged there.

Dr. Wilmut said in the telephone interview last week that the method could work for any animal and that he hoped to use it next to clone cattle. He said that he could use many types of cells from adults for cloning but that the easiest to use would be so-called stem cells, which give rise to a variety of other cells and are present throughout the body.

In his sheep experiment, he used mammary cells because a company that sponsored his work, PPL Therapeutics, is developing sheep that can be used to produce proteins that can be used as drugs in their milk, so it had sheep mammary cells readily available.

For Dr. Wilmut, the main interest of the experiment is to advance animal research. PPL, for example, wants to clone animals that can produce pharmacologically useful proteins, like the clotting factor needed by hemophiliacs. Scientists would grow cells in the laboratory, insert the genes for production of the desired protein, select those cells that most actively churned out the protein and use those cells to make cloned females. The cloned animals would produce immense amounts of the proteins in their milk, making the animals into living drug factories.

But that is only the beginning, Dr. Wilmut said. Researchers could use the same method to make animals with human diseases, like cystic fibrosis, and then test therapies on the cloned animals. Or they could use cloning to alter the proteins on the surfaces of pig organs, like the liver or heart, making the organs more like human organs. Then they could transplant those organs into humans.

Dr. First said the "exciting and astounding" cloning result could shake the dairy industry. It could allow the cloning of cows that are superproducers of milk, making 30,000 or even 40,000 pounds of milk a year. The average cow makes about 13,000 pounds of milk a year, he said.

"I think that if — and it's a very big if — cloning were highly efficient," Dr. First said last week, "then it could be a more significant revolution to the livestock industry than even artificial insemination."

Although Dr. Wilmut said he saw no intrinsic biological reason humans, too, could not be cloned, he dismissed the idea as being ethically unacceptable. Moreover, he said, it is illegal in Britain to clone people. "I would find it offensive," to clone a human being, Dr. Wilmut said, adding that he fervently hoped that no one would try it.

But others said that it was hard to imagine enforcing a ban on cloning people when cloning got more efficient. "I could see it going on surreptitiously," said Lori Andrews, a professor at Chicago-Kent College of law who specializes in reproductive issues. For example, Professor Andrews said last week, in the early days of in vitro fertilization, Australia banned that practice. "So scientists moved to Singapore" and offered the procedure, she said. "I can imagine new crimes," she added.

People might be cloned without their knowledge or consent. After all, all that would be needed would be some cells. If there is a market for a sperm bank selling semen from Nobel laureates, how much better would it be to bear a child that would actually be a clone of a great thinker or, perhaps, a great beauty or great athlete?

"The genie is out of the bottle," said Dr. Ronald Munson, a medical ethicist at the University of Missouri in St. Louis. "This technology is not, in principle, policeable."

Dr. Munson called the possibilities incredible. For example, could researchers devise ways to add just the DNA of an adult cell, without fusing two living cells? If so, might it be possible to clone the dead?

"I had an idea for a story once," Dr. Munson said, in which a scientist obtains a spot of blood from the cross on which Jesus was crucified. He then uses it to clone a man who is Jesus Christ — or perhaps cannot be.

On a more practical note, Dr. Munson mused over the strange twist that science has taken.

"There's something ironic" about the study, he said. "Here we have this incredible technical accomplishment, and what motivated it? The desire for more sheep milk of a certain type." It is, he said, "the theater of the absurd acted out by scientists."

In his interview with the Press Association, Britain's domestic news agency, Dr. Wilmut added early today: "We are aware that there is potential for misuse, and we have provided information to ethicists and the Human Embryology Authority. We believe that it is important that society decides how we want to use this technology and makes sure it prohibits what it wants to prohibit. It would be desperately sad if people started using this sort of technology with people."

CHAPTER 5

Treatments Never Before Seen: 2000–Present

As the new millennium dawns, medical advances that once seemed like science fiction are now possible. DNA is revealed as the blueprint of the human animal. The entire human genome is mapped for the first time, and certain cancer–causing genes are identified. Cloning creates stem cells with the power to further medical science, despite ethical concerns. Medical devices like the pacemaker debut and evolve, eventually utilizing robots and artificial intelligence. Vaccines continue to be developed against viruses, including the HIV virus. Medical marijuana gains grudging acceptance for its therapeutic benefits.

Once Again, Scientists Say Human Genome Is Complete

BY NICHOLAS WADE | APRIL 15, 2003

THE HUMAN GENOME is complete and the Human Genome Project is over, leaders of a public consortium of academic centers said today.

"We have before us the instruction set that carries each of us from the one-cell egg through adulthood to the grave," Dr. Robert Waterston, a leading genome sequencer, said at a news conference here at the National Institutes of Health.

Dr. James D. Watson announces that a six-country consortium has successfully drawn up a complete map of the human genome.

Their announcement marked the end of a scientific venture that began in October 1990 and was expected to take 15 years.

Today's finishing date, two years ahead of schedule, was timed to coincide with the 50th anniversary of the discovery of the structure of DNA by Dr. James D. Watson and Dr. Francis Crick. Their article appeared in the April 25, 1953, issue of Nature.

Dr. Watson, who became the first director of the Human Genome Project at the institutes, was at a conference here today to celebrate the genome's completion. He had sought that goal, he said, realizing that a family member's illness would never be treatable "until we understand the human program for health and disease."

A "working draft" of the human genome sequence was announced with much fanfare three years ago in a White House ceremony. But at that stage the Human Genome Project had completed only 85 percent of the genome and its commercial rival, the Celera Corporation, using the project's data as well as its own, had attained somewhat more. The project's draft was not a thing of beauty. It consisted of thousands of short segments of DNA, whose order and orientation in the full genome was largely unknown.

Three years later, the international consortium of genome sequencing centers has now put all the fragments in order and closed most of the gaps, producing an extensive and highly accurate sequence of the 3.1 billion units of DNA of the human genome.

The data, perceived as the foundation of a new era of medicine, will be posted for free on genetic data banks. Celera, whose data are available by subscription, never intended to carry its draft genome to completion.

The working draft of three years ago contained most human genes and was useful for researchers seeking a specific gene. But up to a year ago biologists said they often had to do considerable extra sequencing work on the DNA regions they were interested in.

The completed genome announced today is far more accurate. It can be used out of the box, so to speak, without extra resequencing. The genes and other important elements of the genome are now almost all in their correct position, a vital requirement for researchers seeking to locate a gene that contributes to disease.

Scientists praised the Human Genome Project for its further three years of hard work and for producing a resource of enormous value to research. But several qualified their admiration by noting that even if the project is complete, the human genome is not. The parts of the genome still missing are of minor importance, but many biologists would like to see them sequenced before declaring the genome finished.

The human genome is packaged in 23 pairs of chromosomes, each a giant molecule of DNA. Though DNA's best-known role is to encode the information needed to build specific proteins, the working parts of the living cell, some of the DNA performs structural roles. This includes the DNA at the tips of each chromosome and at the center. The tip and center DNA, known as heterochromatic DNA, consists of monotonously repeated sequences whose exact order of units is so hard to determine that the consortium's leaders said from the outset they would not try to do so.

Within the rest of the DNA, known as euchromatic DNA, some regions are very hard to sequence for technical reasons. For example, they may contain DNA that is toxic to the bacteria used to amplify them. Foreseeing such difficult regions, the consortium said it would accept some gaps in the eventual sequence, provided their length was known.

When the working draft of the human genome was produced, consortium scientists called it the "Book of Life," with each chromosome a chapter. In the edition published today, small sections at the beginning, end and middle of each chapter are blank, along with some 400 assorted paragraphs whose text is missing, although the length of the missing passages is known.

The missing paragraphs amount to only 0.8 percent of the euchromatic DNA, which is 2.9 billion base pairs, or DNA units, in length. The total length of the genome, with heterochromatic DNA included, is 3.1 billion base pairs. Because most of the chromosomes have only just been completed — the laggards straggled in only last week — genome analysts have not yet had time to compute the exact number of human genes, put at around 30,000 in earlier estimates.

Dr. Francis Collins, director of the genome center at the National Institutes of Health, said the Human Genome Project had completed the task it set itself and was today dissolved. The era of large-scale DNA sequencing was now over, he said, although research projects would continue to develop technology to close remaining gaps. "If you are looking for a disease gene you can be confident that it exists in one continuous stretch of highly accurate sequence," he said of the genome data now available.

Dr. Huntington F. Willard, an expert on the X chromosome at Duke, said that the human genome sequence now available was "a momentous achievement" but that "we shouldn't declare the job 'complete' until it is." He said it was "critical that the complete human genome sequence be, well, complete, in the fullness of time."

Dr. Evan Eichler, a computational biologist at Case Western Reserve University who studies certain duplicated regions of the genome, said, "For the vast majority of users, this is in fact an operational completion." But, like Dr. Willard, he said work on the genome should continue until "every base is completely in place." The task might take 10 to 20 years, he said, and he expressed concern that the effort might not be sustained.

A prime beneficiary of the essentially completed genome is DeCode Genetics of Reykjavik, Iceland, which is screening the entire Icelandic population for disease-causing variant genes. Dr. Kari Stefansson, the president of the company, said the single base variants known as SNP's were now accurately assigned on the genome sequence 99 percent of the time, compared with 93 percent accuracy previously. The SNP's, which make one person's genome different from another's, are helpful in pinpointing errant genes providing that the position of the SNP's on the genome is known with accuracy.

Dr. Stefansson said the current version of the human genome was "absolutely wonderful to have" but that it was "silly" to claim it was completed.

Two laboratory organisms whose genomes were sequenced as pilot projects for the human genome, the C. elegans roundworm and the Drosophila fruit fly, are in a more complete state than the human genome. Every single base of the roundworm genome is known. Dr. Gerald M. Rubin of the Howard Hughes Medical Institute in Chevy Chase, Md., who oversees the fruit fly project, said that the human genome could not be called finished but that there has been "a tremendous increase in the value" of the sequence over the last two years. "The people who stayed in the trenches deserve a lot of credit, even though the glory may have been claimed by others," he said.

The principal contributors to the human genome sequence are the Sanger Institute near Cambridge in England, which has done 30 percent of the sequence, the Whitehead Institute in Cambridge, Mass., and the Genome Sequencing Center at Washington University in St. Louis. Other contributors include the Baylor College of Medicine, the Department of Energy's Joint Genome Institute, and centers in Japan, France, Germany and China.

Dr. Richard Wilson, director of the Washington University center, said the hardest chromosome had been the Y chromosome, which is small but has many highly repetitive sequences that are hard to tell apart. In Chromosome 7, the individual being sequenced possesses a gene not found in other people, Dr. Wilson said.

The sequence of each of the 24 human chromosomes was put together by a chromosome coordinator. Each coordinator's work was checked against independent data developed by Dr. David Jaffe and Dr. Eric Lander at the Whitehead Institute.

The Human Genome Project was originally projected to cost a total of $3 billion. Money spent by the National Institutes of Health and the Department of Energy since the beginning of the project has come to $2.7 billion, but that does not include spending by the Sanger Institute and other foreign collaborators.

The total spending of the Human Genome Project includes pilot projects like sequencing the roundworm and fruit fly genomes. No exact figure was given at today's press conference for sequencing the human genome specifically. But the Sanger Institute has spent 150 million pounds, or about $235 million, to sequence 30 percent of the genome, and on that basis would have required 500 million pounds, or $786 million at the current rate of exchange, to do all of it.

Though the Human Genome Project has been declared completed, the genome sequencing centers will not go out of business. They have switched to decoding the genomes of other species, and to exploring variations in the human genome.

Obtaining the sequence of the human genome is a first step. Biologists must now annotate it, or identify the regions of DNA that hold the genes and their control elements. Next come tasks like discovering the variations in DNA sequence that contribute to disease in different populations, defining the proteins produced by each gene, and understanding how the proteins in each cell interact in a circuitry that controls the operation of the genome.

First Face Transplant Performed in the U.S.

BY LAWRENCE K. ALTMAN | DEC. 16, 2008

CLEVELAND CLINIC SURGEONS have performed the nation's first near total face transplant, officials said on Tuesday. The patient is a woman who was not identified.

Three partial face transplants have been performed since 2005, two in France and one in China. All have involved using facial tissue from a dead donor with permission from their families. The Cleveland surgical team, led by Dr. Maria Siemionow, said it had replaced about 80 percent of the patient's face with that of a dead woman in the last two weeks. The doctors offered no details on the patient, but said they would discuss her surgery at a news conference on Wednesday.

Recent improvements in managing the care of transplant surgical patients, including the use of better anti-rejection drugs, have allowed doctors to forge into new areas of tissue transplants, including the hands and face.

Such transplants are experimental and highly controversial.

A main area of concern, critics contend, is that the recipients must take anti-rejection drugs for the rest of their lives. An adverse reaction can come at any time, but can often be managed by adjusting the dose of the drugs. But such fine-tuning involves a balancing act — giving sufficient amounts of the drugs to prevent rejection of the tissue but not enough to lead to infection. What can make a face transplant particularly risky is that, if the drugs fail, surgeons may have little to offer the recipient.

Critics have also raised ethical concerns, including protecting the donor's identity. Plans for face transplants at a number of medical centers in this country and Europe have been slowed by difficulty in finding donors.

But transplant pioneers say that the psychological effects of facial damage from injuries, birth defects, burns and a number of diseases can be psychologically devastating. Though reconstructive surgery is possible in many cases, proponents say that in other cases, an experimental face transplant could be worth the risks if patients and donors and their families understand them.

Transplant surgery pioneers also point to the apparent success of the three earlier face transplants and a number of hand transplants. Some of these operations — so-called composite transplants — have involved transplanting not only the skin, but also underlying soft tissues.

In November 2005, a team in Amiens, France, performed the first partial face transplant. The recipient, Isabelle Dinoire, then 38, was seriously disfigured when her Labrador retriever mauled her. The surgeons grafted a nose, lips and chin from a donor who had been declared brain dead.

In a published report in December 2007, Ms. Dinoire's doctors said she was satisfied with the aesthetic result. She has spoken in a news conference.

In 2006, Chinese doctors did a partial face transplant on a farmer who lost much of the right side of his face in a bear attack.

In 2007, a French team performed the third partial facial transplant, on a 29-year-old man. His face had been disfigured by neurofibromatosis, a genetic disorder of the nervous system that causes tumors to grow in tissues around nerves.

Cloning Is Used to Create Embryonic Stem Cells

BY ANDREW POLLACK | MAY 15, 2013

SCIENTISTS HAVE FINALLY succeeded in using cloning to create human embryonic stem cells, a step toward developing replacement tissue to treat diseases but one that might also hasten the day when it will be possible to create cloned babies.

The researchers, at Oregon Health and Science University, took skin cells from a baby with a genetic disease and fused them with donated human eggs to create human embryos that were genetically identical to the 8-month-old. They then extracted stem cells from those embryos.

The embryo-creation technique is essentially the same as that used to create Dolly the sheep and the many cloned animals that have followed. In those cases, the embryos were implanted in the wombs of surrogate mothers.

The Oregon researchers, led by Prof. Shoukhrat Mitalipov, did not implant their human embryos and said they had no intention of doing so. They say their technique, in any case, would not lead to the birth of a viable baby. The same technique, tried in monkeys for years, never resulted in the birth of a cloned monkey, they said.

Nonetheless, the fact that the scientists were able to get cloned human embryos to survive long enough for stem cell extraction is likely to be seen as a step on the way to human reproductive cloning.

The Conference of Catholic Bishops, for instance, said Wednesday that the research "will be taken up by those who want to produce cloned children as 'copies' of other people."

Cardinal Sean O'Malley of Boston said human cloning was immoral, even if used for therapeutic purposes, because it "treats human being as products, manufactured to order to suit other people's wishes."

The Oregon researchers, who published a paper on their work in the journal Cell, say their goal is what has been called therapeutic cloning: making embryonic stem cells that are genetically identical to a particular patient.

Embryonic stem cells can turn into any type of cell in the body, like heart cells, muscles or neurons. That raises the hope that one day the cells will be turned into replacement tissue or even replacement organs to treat a host of diseases.

Human embryonic cells are now mainly derived from embryos created by fertilization in fertility clinics. But tissues created from those stem cells would not genetically match a patient, meaning steps might be needed to prevent rejection.

Scientists have been trying for more than 10 years to create human embryonic stem cells using the cloning method. Korean researchers made international headlines in 2005 when they claimed to have done this, but the claim turned out to be fraudulent.

Still, the demand for therapeutic cloning may be less now than it was a decade ago because scientists can now use adult skin cells to create a stem cell very similar to embryonic cells, but without the need for embryos. These are called induced pluripotent stem cells. The induced cells also sidestep the ethical issues of embryonic stem cells, which are often created by destroying embryos.

Attempts to use either type of cell for therapy remain at the early stages of research, so it is not clear which will turn out to be better. So-called adult stem cells, taken from blood, fat or other parts of the body, are another possible option.

Dr. Mitalipov and his colleagues created monkey stem cells through cloning in 2007 and since then have been trying to tweak the technique to work with human cells.

A drawback of therapeutic cloning is that there might never be enough human eggs available to treat all patients, should the therapy ever work. Egg donors can suffer serious side effects from the powerful hormones needed to generate multiple eggs.

Dr. Mitalipov said the technique was efficient enough that one donation — which can include multiple eggs — would probably be enough to generate a stem cell line, even accounting for failures.

Most patients who would want replacement tissues are likely to be old. The researchers must still show they can produce stem cells starting with skin cells from adults.

Google and Johnson & Johnson Team for Robotic Surgery Projects

BY CONOR DOUGHERTY | MARCH 27, 2015

GOOGLE WANTS TO be everywhere, even inside your body.

On Friday, Google and the pharmaceutical giant Johnson & Johnson announced a partnership between Google's life sciences division and Ethicon, a division of Johnson & Johnson that makes surgical products, to develop new robot-assisted surgery technologies.

The deal "will help explore how the latest innovations in computer science and advanced imaging and sensors could be integrated into tools that help surgeons as they operate," Google said in a statement.

For now, the announcement is mostly just that — an announcement. The companies gave few details about the nature of the partnership or how much money might be involved. Google at least said its contribution would not be in developing surgical instruments, but rather in its particular skill in handling large amounts of data.

In statements, the companies suggested that some of their goals included developing imaging technologies that would give surgeons a clearer real-time look inside the body, or software that could highlight features that are crucial but difficult to see, such as blood vessels, nerves or the margins around a tumor, which can be crucial to a successful cancer surgery.

Google also said its team would try to figure out how to consolidate volumes of medical data and testing into a more useful interface.

"Surgeons typically consult multiple separate screens in the operating room to view preoperative medical images (e.g., M.R.I.s), see results of previous surgeries and lab tests, or understand how to navigate an aberrant anatomical structure," the company said in its statement. "Smart software could overlay these images on top of the interface where a surgeon is already viewing a robotic-assisted operation."

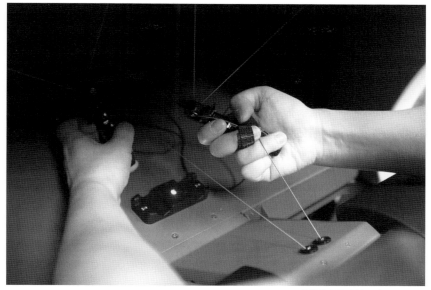

Doctors perform a surgery with a "da Vinci" surgical robot at Wuhan Tongji Hospital last month in Wuhan, China.

Google has ambitions far beyond Internet search, and over the last year, biotechnology has become one of its favorite areas to explore. The company created its life sciences division, which is part of its Google X research unit, with the 2013 hiring of Andrew Conrad, a molecular biologist who is head of the division.

Mr. Conrad's steadily growing team has announced several projects that sound like science fiction, including a contact lens that can measure glucose levels, a longevity project called the Baseline Study and an attempt to create a pill with particles the size of molecules that would be able to detect diseases like cancer.

In addition to the life sciences division, Google has also joined with Arthur D. Levinson, a former chief executive of Genentech, to create a pharmaceutical company called Calico. Last year, Calico announced that it would build a new Bay Area facility that will research diseases that afflict the elderly, such as neurodegeneration and cancer.

Robot-assisted surgeries have become a rapidly growing area of medicine, but big questions exist about their cost and safety. In particular, the effectiveness of the "da Vinci" surgical robot has been questioned in studies and dubbed "fake innovation" by critics.

Last year, the National Science Foundation teamed with private donors and scientists at the University of California, Berkeley, to establish a research center to help develop a second generation of medical robots that could perform low-level and repetitive surgical tasks.

Prosthetic Limbs, Controlled by Thought

BY THE NEW YORK TIMES | MAY 20, 2015

ENGINEERS AT THE Johns Hopkins University Applied Physics Lab have developed a next-generation prosthetic: a robotic arm that has 26 joints, can curl up to 45 pounds and is controlled with a person's mind just like a regular arm.

Researchers think the arm could help people like Les Baugh, who lost both arms at the shoulder after an electrical accident as a teenager. Now 59, Mr. Baugh recently underwent surgery at Johns Hopkins to remap the remaining nerves from his missing arms, allowing brain signals to be sent to the prosthetic.

Mr. Baugh's custom socket can pick up brain signals to control the arms, known as Modular Prosthetic Limbs, or M.P.L., just by thinking about the movements.

Mike McLoughlin, the chief engineer of research and exploratory development at the lab, said that as the remapped nerves grew deeper, it was possible that Mr. Baugh would feel some sensation in his prostheses. Each arm has over 100 sensors, and other amputees who have had the same surgery reported being able to feel texture through the M.P.L.

Patients of varying disabilities have tested the arm in the lab and helped push the design forward.

The limb is modular, which means it can be broken off or built up to accommodate people with different needs — from a hand amputee to someone missing an entire arm. Quadriplegics or stroke survivors, who have lost the ability to move all or part of their bodies, can also use it as a surrogate arm.

But while the limb is fully functional, it still faces hurdles before making its way outside the lab. It will need approval from the Food and Drug Administration, which could mean a clinical trial.

Mr. McLoughlin also said the cost of the arm needed to be about a tenth of its current price to be viable in the marketplace. There are now about 10 fully functioning M.P.L.s, and each one costs an estimated $500,000.

"We've designed a Maserati here, but what most people will want is a good Toyota," Mr. McLoughlin said. "The M.P.L. was intentionally designed to be as sophisticated as we could make it so that you could really push the state of the art, but ultimately for commercializing it, it needs to be a lower cost design."

Since 2006, the lab has been awarded $120 million from a program run by the Pentagon's Defense Advanced Research Projects Agency to help wounded warriors. The lab worked with technology developer and manufacturer HDT Global to make a prosthetic that mimics the human arm in dexterity and strength.

"The long-term goal for all of this work is to have noninvasive — no extra surgeries, no extra implants — ways to control a dexterous robotic device," said Robert Armiger, project manager for amputee research at the Johns Hopkins lab. In the future, researchers envision a kind of cap with sensors that an amputee or paralyzed person could wear that would feed information about brain activity to the robotic arm.

The lab is starting to collaborate with industry partners to explore commercial opportunities. They hope the Modular Prosthetic Limb, or a version of it, will be available to consumers within a few years.

— *Emma Cott*

Veterans Groups Push for Medical Marijuana to Treat PTSD

BY REGGIE UGWU | NOV. 3, 2017

AMONG CRITICS OF the federal prohibition of marijuana — a diverse and bipartisan group that includes both criminal justice reform advocates and Big Alcohol — the American Legion and its allies stand out.

For more than a year, the stalwart veterans group has been working to reframe the debate as a question of not only moral and economic imperatives, but also patriotic ones, arguing that access to medical marijuana could ease suffering and reduce suicide rates among soldiers who return from the horrors of war.

"We've got young men and women with PTSD and traumatic brain injuries coming to us and saying that cannabis works," Joe Plenzler, a spokesman for the group, which was established after World War I and has over two million members, said by telephone Wednesday.

Mr. Plenzler said that veterans had turned to medical marijuana as an alternative to so-called "zombie drugs," including opioids and antidepressants, that they said adversely affected their mood and personality, up to and including thoughts of suicide. In studies, cannabis has been shown to help alleviate chronic pain and reduce muscle spasms in multiple sclerosis patients.

In 2016, the American Legion petitioned the government to relax federal restrictions on marijuana in two ways. The group asked Congress to remove the drug from the list of Schedule 1 narcotics — a class that includes heroin, LSD and other drugs that have "no accepted medical use" and a high potential for abuse — and reclassify it in a lower schedule. It also called on the Drug Enforcement Administration to license more privately funded growers to focus on medical research.

Because marijuana is a Schedule 1 drug, there is surprisingly little rigorous research into its medical applications, as researchers have found themselves stymied by regulatory hurdles at federal health and drug agencies and short on a supply of federally approved product.

The classification also means that veterans — many of whom rely on the federal Veterans Affairs Department for their health care — cannot get coverage for medical marijuana, even in the 29 states that have legalized it.

On Thursday, The American Legion published a phone survey of over 800 veterans and veteran caregivers in which 92 percent of respondents said they supported research into medical cannabis for the purpose of treating mental or physical conditions. Eighty-two percent said they wanted cannabis as a federally legal treatment option.

"Even in the states where it's legal, there's still the stigma associated with the federal ban," said Louis Celli, the group's national director of veterans affairs and rehabilitation. He noted that soldiers were regularly subjected to urinalysis and told to stay away from the drug. "It puts veterans in a very difficult position."

Though a Quinnipiac University poll released in April found that a record 94 percent of all Americans supported doctor-prescribed medical marijuana usage, veterans advocating research have run into the same roadblock as pro-cannabis activists around the country: the Justice Department.

President Trump campaigned in support of medical marijuana and said that recreational usage should be a "state-by-state" issue. But his attorney general, Jeff Sessions, has been an outspoken critic of legalizing the drug for any purpose. Veterans groups draw a straight line from obstacles to medical marijuana research to the doorstep of Mr. Sessions.

"He is putting politics, antiquated policies and his own personal opinion ahead of the health needs of veterans in this country," said Nick Etten, executive director of Veterans Cannabis Project, referring to Mr. Sessions.

Marijuana being trimmed at a farm in California. The American Legion asked Congress to remove the drug from the list of Schedule 1 narcotics.

A representative for the Justice Department declined to comment, but Mr. Sessions said during an oversight hearing with the Senate Judiciary Committee last month that he was considering expanding the supply of research-grade marijuana.

Veterans groups say the fastest and most effective way to help veterans get access to treatment is to simply reschedule the drug. That would automatically lift the most onerous barriers to research and allow V.A. health care providers to immediately prescribe marijuana in states where it is legal.

But getting the necessary legislation through a fractious, conservative congress may still be a pipe dream.

Representative Matt Gaetz of Florida is one of a growing number of Republicans who have joined Democrats in trying to formally recast the government's stance on marijuana. With Darren Soto, Democrat of Florida, Mr. Gaetz was co-author of a bill that would bump the drug down to Schedule 3 — the same classification as codeine and anabolic steroids.

"I think my political party became too committed to this antiquated dogma of the '70s and '80s," Mr. Gaetz said, referring to a time when cannabis was widely considered to be a "gateway" to more harmful drugs.

"Now we're having to pull the ostrich's head out of the sand."

Nearly 21 Million Now Receiving AIDS Drugs, U.N. Agency Says

BY DONALD G. MCNEIL JR. | NOV. 20, 2017

ALMOST 21 MILLION PEOPLE around the world are now getting life-prolonging AIDS drugs, according to a report issued on Monday. But another 16 million people infected with H.I.V. are not yet on medication.

The report was released in South Africa by Unaids, the joint United Nations AIDS-fighting agency.

Antiretroviral triple therapy became standard in wealthy countries in 1996, but it took almost a decade for just one million people in poor countries to receive treatment.

That happened only after generic drugs became available and donor organizations like the Global Fund to Fight AIDS, Tuberculosis and Malaria were created to pay for them.

Unaids has set a goal called "90-90-90" by 2020. That is: 90 percent of the world's H.I.V.-infected people having had an H.I.V. test; 90 percent of those who test positive having been prescribed drugs; and 90 percent of those prescribed drugs staying on them faithfully enough to have undetectable levels of the virus in their blood.

After "remarkable progress" toward that goal, the world is now at "70-77-82," the agency said.

But that means that only 44 percent of the world's H.I.V.-infected people are virally suppressed — that is, that they are taking medication consistently enough to provide a nearly normal life span.

By that measure, the countries doing best are Botswana, Britain, Cambodia, Denmark, Iceland, Singapore and Sweden.

The report also notes a few cities doing especially well: Amsterdam, Melbourne, New York, Paris and San Francisco.

Only four countries in Africa — where the epidemic has hit hardest — are getting drugs to even 75 percent of their citizens needing them: Botswana, Rwanda, Swaziland and Zimbabwe.

The number of people dying of AIDS annually peaked in 2005, at about two million. Now, about half that number die each year, but AIDS is still the leading cause of death for women in their childbearing years.

The number of "AIDS orphans" — children and teenagers whose parents have died — peaked at 20 million in 2009. It is declining but still stands at about 16 million.

Dr. Adel Mahmoud, Who Was Credited With HPV and Rotavirus Vaccines, Dies at 76

OBITUARY | BY DENISE GRADY | JUNE 19, 2018

DR. ADEL MAHMOUD, an infectious-disease expert who played a vital role in the development of lifesaving vaccines, died on June 11 in Manhattan. He was 76.

His death, at Mount Sinai St. Luke's Hospital, was caused by a brain hemorrhage, his wife, Dr. Sally Hodder, said.

As president of Merck Vaccines from 1998 until 2006, Dr. Mahmoud oversaw the creation and marketing of several vaccines that brought major advances in public health. One prevents rotavirus infection, a potentially fatal cause of diarrhea in babies. Another protects against human papillomavirus (HPV), which causes cancers of the cervix, anus, genitals and middle of the throat.

Dr. Mahmoud also helped usher in a combination vaccine against measles, mumps, rubella and chickenpox, and one to prevent shingles, the painful and debilitating illness that can develop when a previous chickenpox infection is reactivated.

The rotavirus and HPV vaccines were contentious subjects and might never have reached the market without Dr. Mahmoud's determination, said Dr. Julie L. Gerberding, an executive vice president at Merck & Co., and former head of the federal Centers for Disease Control and Prevention. She joined Merck after Dr. Mahmoud retired but described him as a "lifelong mentor."

Dr. Mahmoud championed those vaccines because he recognized their potential to save lives, she said. Globally, cervical cancer and rotavirus infections kill hundreds of thousands of women and children every year.

The problem with a rotavirus vaccine was that another company had already developed one but then had to take it off the market because it was found to increase the risk of bowel obstruction in infants. Opponents argued that it would take a large study and a huge investment of time and money to test Merck's candidate vaccine, and then to overcome public fears.

"Everyone wanted to kill it," Dr. Gerberding said. "Adel said, 'Not only are we going to do it, but we're going to make our study even larger to prove it works and is safe.' "

Dr. Mahmoud took a similar approach to the HPV vaccine, which also had its detractors. Some doubted that it would work. Others thought parents would reject it, fearing that vaccinating young girls would somehow encourage them to start having sex. That fear was based on the virus's being sexually transmitted and the view that the vaccine was most effective if given before girls become sexually active.

Dr. Mahmoud prevailed, and Merck's HPV vaccine, Gardasil, approved in 2006, was the first to be marketed.

Last month, in a call to eliminate cervical cancer worldwide, the head of the World Health Organization called HPV vaccines "truly wonderful inventions" and said all girls should be given them.

Dr. Anthony S. Fauci, director of the National Institute of Allergy and Infectious Diseases, said he had called on Dr. Mahmoud many times to advise his institute.

"He clearly had a knack for understanding the big picture," Dr. Fauci said. "He was a 40,000-foot kind of guy, who could understand areas of science, research, policy and clinical medicine well beyond his own specific designated area of expertise."

Dr. Mahmoud also had "an amazingly likable personality," Dr. Fauci said.

"Even though he was dead serious when advising you on important matters, he had this effervescent, bubbling personality," he added.

Adel Mahmoud was born on Aug. 24, 1941, in Cairo, the eldest of three children. His father, Abdelfattah Mahmoud, was an agricultural engineer. His mother, Fathia Osman, did not work outside the home, though she had hoped to study medicine and had been accepted by the University of Cairo's medical school. Her brother, a medical student, had stopped her from attending because he did not think women should be doctors.

A boyhood experience had a profound influence on Dr. Mahmoud. When he was 10, his father contracted pneumonia, and young Adel was sent to the drugstore for penicillin. He ran home with it only to find that his father had died. As the eldest son, he was now head of the family.

"I often wondered if his strength as a leader and his clear vision originated from being forced into those roles at an early age," his wife, Dr. Hodder, said.

Dr. Mahmoud studied medicine at the University of Cairo, graduating in 1963. He left Egypt for Britain in 1968 and earned a doctorate from the London School of Hygiene and Tropical Medicine in 1971. He did research on diseases caused by parasitic worms and the role of a certain type of blood cell in the body's efforts to defend itself.

Dr. Mahmoud emigrated to the United States in 1973 as a postdoctoral fellow at Case Western Reserve University in Cleveland. He later led the university's division of geographic medicine and was chairman of the department of medicine from 1987 to 1998.

He met Dr. Hodder there in 1976, and they married in 1993. She is also an infectious-disease specialist.

Merck recruited Dr. Mahmoud in 1998. He retired from the company in 2006, and then became a professor at the Woodrow Wilson School of Public and International Affairs and the department of molecular biology at Princeton University.

In 2013, when an unusual strain of meningitis caused an outbreak on campus — one for which there was no vaccine made in the United States — Dr. Mahmoud used his expertise, powers of persuasion and connections in the pharmaceutical world to help the university acquire a European vaccine and obtain permission from the government to offer it to students on an emergency basis.

After the Ebola outbreak in West Africa in 2014, Dr. Mahmoud began advocating the creation of a global vaccine-development fund.

In addition to his wife, he is survived by a stepson, Jay Thornton; his sister, Dr. Olfat Abdelfattah; and his brother, Dr. Mahmoud Abdelfattah.

Immune-Based Treatment Helps Fight Aggressive Breast Cancer, Study Finds

BY DENISE GRADY | OCT. 20, 2018

WOMEN WITH AN aggressive type of breast cancer lived longer if they received immunotherapy plus chemotherapy, rather than chemo alone, a major study has found.

The results are expected to change the standard of care for women like those in the clinical trial, who had advanced cases of "triple-negative" breast cancer. That form of the disease often resists standard therapies, and survival rates are poor. It is twice as common in African-American women as in white women, and more likely to occur in younger women.

Researchers said the new study was a long-awaited breakthrough for immunotherapy in breast cancer. Until now, most progress had been in other cancers, including lung cancer and melanoma, an aggressive skin cancer.

These findings may lead to the first approval by the Food and Drug Administration for an immunotherapy drug to treat breast cancer. But the approval would likely be limited to a certain type of aggressive cancer.

Although triple-negative tumors occur in only about 15 percent of patients with invasive breast cancer in the United States (or nearly 40,000 each year), they account for a disproportionate share of deaths, as many as 30 percent to 40 percent.

"These women really needed a break," Dr. Ingrid Mayer, a breast cancer specialist at Vanderbilt University, said in a telephone interview. "Nothing has worked well."

Dr. Mayer, who was not part of the study, called the findings "very significant." She said she had received consulting fees from seven drug companies, including Genentech, which is the maker of the immunotherapy drug in the study and paid for the research.

The term triple-negative refers to the tumors' lack of sensitivity to the hormones estrogen and progesterone, and their lack of a protein called HER2, which is a target of treatment.

The immunotherapy in the study was atezolizumab (brand name Tecentriq), which belongs to a class of drugs called checkpoint inhibitors; the chemotherapy was nab-paclitaxel (Abraxane).

The findings were published on Saturday in The New England Journal of Medicine, and were to be presented at a meeting of the European Society for Medical Oncology, in Munich. The study included 902 patients treated at 246 medical centers in 41 countries. Genentech, which is part of Roche, has already submitted the data to the F.D.A. for approval.

Checkpoint inhibitors like atezolizumab work by helping T-cells — a type of white blood cell that is part of the immune system — recognize cancer and attack it. Research that led to these drugs won this year's Nobel Prize in medicine.

The drugs generally work for fewer than half of patients but can bring lasting recoveries even to people who were severely ill. Side effects can be dangerous, even life-threatening, and treatment costs more than $100,000 a year.

In other cancers, researchers sometimes describe the tumors as "hot," meaning they tend to have many mutations — genetic abnormalities that the immune system can recognize as foreign and attack.

But breast cancers tend to be relatively "cold," with fewer mutations. The immune system is less likely to recognize them as invaders, which may help explain why previous studies of checkpoint inhibitors in breast cancer have been somewhat disappointing, researchers say.

In the new study, the key to success seems to have been giving chemotherapy along with immunotherapy.

"Chemo takes away the invisibility cloak the cancer has managed to put on," Dr. Mayer said.

The chemo may help to ignite the immune system, in part by killing cancer cells that then spill substances the T-cells detect as foreign and begin to hunt.

The new study "is a big deal and has been the buzz of the breast cancer research world," said Dr. Larry Norton of Memorial Sloan Kettering Cancer Center in an email. He was not involved in the study, although he said he had done paid consulting work for the past two years for the maker of Abraxane.

Beyond changing treatment practices, he said the research "opens the door to new approaches to harness the immune system to fight breast cancer, and there is every reason to expect major advances there."

He cautioned that the combined treatment would have to be studied further, to assess side effects.

Dr. Kevin Kalinsky, a breast cancer specialist at NewYork-Presbyterian/Columbia University Irving Medical Center, suggested that patients like those in the study should talk to their doctors "about whether it is possible for them to get access to the medication while we're waiting for F.D.A. approval."

He did not take part in this study. He said he has received consulting fees from about 10 drug companies, including Genentech.

The women in the study had triple-negative breast cancer that had been newly diagnosed and had become metastatic, meaning it had begun to spread. Once that occurs, the outlook is grim, with many patients surviving 18 months or less.

Half received chemo alone, and half were given chemo plus immunotherapy.

Among those who received the combination, the median survival was 21.3 months, compared with 17.6 months for those who received chemo alone. The difference was not statistically significant.

But when the researchers looked at women who had a marker called PD-L1 on their cancer cells, the results were striking: The median survival was 25 months in the combination group, versus 15.5 months with just chemo. That finding has not been analyzed statistically, and the patients are still being followed.

Doctors say the survival difference is important.

Dr. Sylvia Adams.

"This is truly a game changer," said Dr. Sylvia Adams, an author of the study from NYU Langone Health's Perlmutter Cancer Center.

Cancer patients with the PD-L1 marker tend to respond better to checkpoint inhibitors than those without it. In this study, 41 percent of patients had the marker. Genentech is seeking approval for treatment in triple-negative patients with the marker.

Dr. Adams said some patients, after initial treatment with both types of drug, have been doing well for two or three years with immunotherapy alone.

The "million-dollar question," she said, is whether they can safely stop the immunotherapy if they have no sign of cancer. For the time being, they are sticking with the treatment.

She noted that patients in the study had some of the expected side effects of immunotherapy, including lung and pancreas inflammation.

Dr. Adams said she accepted no money from drug companies, but her medical center did receive money from Genentech to pay for the research.

Maribel Ramos, 42, was being treated at another hospital, which recommended chemo for her advanced triple-negative breast cancer.

"I was very worried because I know with that type of cancer, chemo doesn't work," Ms. Ramos said. She has three daughters: a 23-year-old and 10-year-old twins.

Her sister, a nurse at New York University, told her about the study there, and she began treatment in February 2016. She didn't know it at the time, but she had been picked at random to receive the combined treatment. Within a few months, her tumors began to shrink. Nine months ago, for the first time, a scan found no sign of cancer. She is staying on immunotherapy.

"I just feel so happy that you can live longer," Ms. Ramos said. "I wish that all the ladies that are fighting cancer, especially triple-negative, could get this medicine. I would recommend that all women get a second opinion, and sometimes even a third opinion." She added, "This can save your life."

About 266,120 new cases of invasive breast cancer are expected in women in 2018 in the United States, and 40,920 deaths.

Glossary

AIDS A disease that destroys the human immune system as a result of infection by the HIV virus.

BRCA mutation One of two forms of the breast cancer susceptibility genes that increase the likelihood of cancer.

Diphtheria A contagious disease marked by fever and the obstruction of breathing.

DNA Various nucleic acids in a twisted ladder formation that encode hereditary genes.

genome An organism's complete set of genes.

HIV Human immunodeficiency virus, the virus that causes AIDS.

laparotomy A surgical incision in the abdomen.

measles An infections virus that causes fever and a rash.

M.R.I. Magnetic resonance imaging, a procedure that uses radio waves and magnetic fields to create detailed images inside bodies.

pasteurization The heating of a liquid in order to destroy germs.

prophylactic A means of preventing disease.

prosthetic An artificial body part.

PTSD Post-traumatic stress disorder, a mental disorder affecting individuals who have witnessed traumatic events.

yellow fever An infectious disease transmitted by mosquitoes that causes fever, headache, yellow skin, vomiting, and muscle aches.

Media Literacy Terms

"Media literacy" refers to the ability to access, understand, critically assess and create media. The following terms are important components of media literacy, and they will help you critically engage with the articles in this title.

angle The aspect of a news story that a journalist focuses on and develops.

attribution The method by which a source is identified or by which facts and information are assigned to the person who provided them.

balance Principle of journalism that both perspectives of an argument should be presented in a fair way.

bias A form of prejudice in favor of a certain idea, person or perspective.

byline Name of the writer, usually placed between the headline and the story.

caption Identifying copy for a picture; also called a legend or cutline.

chronological order Method of writing a story presenting the details of the story in the order in which they occurred.

credibility The quality of being trustworthy and believable, said of a journalistic source.

critical review A type of story that describes an event or work of art, such as a theater performance, film, concert, book, restaurant, radio or television program, exhibition or musical piece, and offers critical assessment of its quality and reception.

editorial Article of opinion or interpretation.

feature story Article designed to entertain as well as to inform.

headline Type, usually 18 point or larger, used to introduce a story.

impartiality Principle of journalism that a story should not reflect a journalist's bias and should contain balance.

intention The motive or reason behind something, such as the publication of a news story.

interview story A type of story in which the facts are gathered primarily by interviewing another person or persons.

inverted pyramid A method of writing a story using facts in order of importance, beginning with a lead and then gradually adding paragraphs in order of relevance from most interesting to least interesting.

news story An article or style of expository writing that reports news, generally in a straightforward fashion and without editorial comment.

paraphrase The summary of an individual's words, with attribution, rather than a direct quotation of their exact words.

quotation The use of an individual's exact words indicated by the use of quotation marks and proper attribution.

reliability The quality of being dependable and accurate, said of a journalistic source.

source The origin of the information reported in journalism.

style A distinctive use of language in writing or speech; also a news or publishing organization's rules for consistent use of language with regard to spelling, punctuation, typography and capitalization, usually regimented by a house style guide.

tone A manner of expression in writing or speech.

Media Literacy Questions

1. Identify the various sources cited in the article "Anti-Toxine Distributed" (on page 28). How does the journalist attribute information to each of these sources in the article? How effective are the attributions in helping the reader identify sources?

2. In "Aseptolin a New Remedy" (on page 31), the journalist paraphrases information from Dr. Cyrus Edson. The journalist also quoted Dr. Biggs directly. What are the strengths of the use of a paraphrase as opposed to a direct quote? What are the weaknesses?

3. Compare the headlines of "Modern Wound Treatment." (on page 35) and "Lister's War on Pain and Death" (on page 52). Which is a more compelling headline, and why? How could the less compelling headline be changed to better draw the reader's interest?

4. What type of story is "The Triumphs of Surgery" (on page 42)? Can you identify another article in this collection that is the same type of story? What elements helped you come to your conclusion?

5. Does Van Buren Thorne, M.D., demonstrate the journalistic principle of impartiality in the article "Typhus, War's Dread Ally, Beaten" (on page 71)? If so, how did he do so? If not, what could he have included to make his article more impartial?

6. The article "Horace Wells." (on page 20) is an example of a tribute. Identify how the tone helps convey the journalist's angle on the subject.

7. Does "Virus Character Radically Changed" (on page 106) use multiple sources? What are the strengths of using multiple sources in a journalistic piece?

8. "Immune-Based Treatment Helps Fight Aggressive Breast Cancer, Study Finds" (on page 207) features a photograph. What does this photograph add to the article?

9. "Finds New Remedy for Pneumonia" (on page 85) includes numerous quotes by experts. What are the similarities between the quotes? What are the differences?

10. What is the intention of the article "Biochemist Fears Rise of the Unfit" (on page 136)? How effectively does it achieve its intended purpose?

11. "Doctor's Dilemma: How to Keep Up" (on page 140) includes a number of quotes. What are the benefits of providing readers with direct quotes of an interviewed subject's speech? Is the subject of an interview always a reliable source?

12. Analyze the authors' reporting in "New Homosexual Disorder Worries Health Officials" (on page 165) and "A Likely AIDS Cause, but Still No Cure" (on page 171). Do you think one journalist is more balanced in their reporting than the other? If so, why do you think so?

13. "Scientist Reports First Cloning Ever of Adult Mammal" by Gina Kolata (on page 174) and "Cloning Is Used to Create Embryonic Stem Cells" by Andrew Pollack (on page 189) both deal with the subject of cloning. How do they differ from one another in the information they present? What techniques do they use to convey that information?

Citations

All citations in this list are formatted according to the Modern Language Association's (MLA) style guide.

BOOK CITATION

THE NEW YORK TIMES EDITORIAL STAFF. *Medical Treatments*. New York: New York Times Educational Publishing, 2020.

ONLINE ARTICLE CITATIONS

ALTMAN, LAWRENCE K. "First Face Transplant Performed in the U.S." *The New York Times*, 16 Dec. 2008, www.nytimes.com/2008/12/17/health/17face.html.

ALTMAN, LAWRENCE K. "New Homosexual Disorder Worries Health Officials." *The New York Times*, 11 May 1982, www.nytimes.com/1982/05/11/science /new-homosexual-disorder-worries-health-officials.html.

BOFFEY, PHILIP M. "A Likely Aids Cause, But Still No Cure." *The New York Times*, 29 Apr. 1984, timesmachine.nytimes.com/timesmachine/1984 /04/29/154195.html.

DOUGHERTY, CONOR. "Google and Johnson & Johnson Team for Robotic Surgery Projects." *The New York Times*, 27 Mar. 2015, bits.blogs.nytimes.com/2015/03 /27/google-and-johnson-johnson-team-for-robotic-surgery-projects/.

ENGEL, LEONARD. "Doctor's Dilemma." *The New York Times*, 7 June 1959, timesmachine.nytimes.com/timesmachine/1959/06/07/81932500.html.

GRADY, DENISE. "Dr. Adel Mahmoud, Who Was Credited With HPV and Rotavirus Vaccines, Dies at 76." *The New York Times*, 19 June 2018, www.nytimes.com/2018/06/19/obituaries/dr-adel-mahmoud-76 -dies-credited-with-major-vaccines.html.

GRADY, DENISE. "Immune-Based Treatment Helps Fight Aggressive Breast Cancer, Study Finds." *The New York Times*, 20 Oct. 2018, www.nytimes.com /2018/10/20/health/breast-cancer-immunotherapy.html.

JOHNSTON, RICHARD J. H. "Biochemist Fears Rise of the Unfit." *The New York*

Times, 20 May 1958, timesmachine.nytimes.com/timesmachine/1958/05/20/89099771.html.

JONES, STACY V. "X-Ray of Entire Body Shows Color TV Image." *The New York Times*, 29 Nov. 1975, www.nytimes.com/1975/11/29/archives/xray-of-entire-body-shows-color-tv-image-patents-xray-makes-picture.html.

KOLATA, GINA. "Scientist Reports First Cloning Ever of Adult Mammal." *The New York Times*, 23 Feb. 1997, www.nytimes.com/1997/02/23/us/scientist-reports-first-cloning-ever-of-adult-mammal.html.

LAURENCE, WILLIAM L. "Chemicals Excelling Sulfa Drugs as Germ Killers Are Disclosed." *The New York Times*, 10 Sept. 1943, timesmachine.nytimes.com/timesmachine/1943/09/10/85119788.html.

LAURENCE, WILLIAM L. "Doctors Describe a Heart Reviver." *The New York Times*, 24 Oct. 1950, timesmachine.nytimes.com/timesmachine/1950/10/24/84822692.html.

LAURENCE, WILLIAM L. " 'Giant' Germicide Yielded by Mold." *The New York Times*, 6 May 1941, timesmachine.nytimes.com/timesmachine/1941/05/06/85490194.html.

LAURENCE, WILLIAM L. "Virus Character Radically Changed." *The New York Times*, 19 June 1936, timesmachine.nytimes.com/timesmachine/1936/06/19/93522160.html.

MCNEIL, DONALD G., JR. "Nearly 21 Million Now Receiving AIDS Drugs, U.N. Agency Says." *The New York Times*, 20 Nov. 2017, www.nytimes.com/2017/11/20/health/aids-drugs-united-nations.html.

THE NEWARK ADVERTISER. "Modern Embalming." *The New York Times*, 20 Apr. 1855, timesmachine.nytimes.com/timesmachine/1855/04/20/76459754.html.

THE NEW YORK TIMES. "Anti-Toxine Distributed." *The New York Times*, 26 Nov. 1894, timesmachine.nytimes.com/timesmachine/1894/11/26/106881941.html.

THE NEW YORK TIMES. "Aseptolin a New Remedy." *The New York Times*, 8 Feb. 1896, timesmachine.nytimes.com/timesmachine/1896/02/08/104110772.html.

THE NEW YORK TIMES. "Chemical Is Found to Combat Viruses." *The New York Times*, 11 Feb. 1938, timesmachine.nytimes.com/timesmachine/1938/02/11/101019770.html.

THE NEW YORK TIMES. "Conquest of Pellagra." *The New York Times*, 19 June 1938, timesmachine.nytimes.com/timesmachine/1938/06/19/98152953.html.

THE NEW YORK TIMES. "Fanfare Ushers Verdict on Tests." *The New York Times*, 13 Apr. 1955, timesmachine.nytimes.com/timesmachine/1955/04/13/79387405.html.

THE NEW YORK TIMES. "Fighting Against Contagion in City." *The New York Times*, 28 Nov. 1913, https://timesmachine.nytimes.com/timesmachine/1913/11/28/100289206.html.

THE NEW YORK TIMES. "Find Sun Produces the 4th Vitamine." *The New York Times*, 20 June 1922, https://timesmachine.nytimes.com/timesmachine/1922/06/20/109844622.html.

THE NEW YORK TIMES. "Finds New Remedy for Pneumonia." *The New York Times*, 9 May 1924, https://timesmachine.nytimes.com/timesmachine/1924/05/09/104037419.html.

THE NEW YORK TIMES. "Hails 'Blood Bank' as Transfusion Aid." *The New York Times*, 20 Feb. 1938, timesmachine.nytimes.com/timesmachine/1938/02/20/512883882.html.

THE NEW YORK TIMES. "Horace Wells." *The New York Times*, 23 May 1873, timesmachine.nytimes.com/timesmachine/1873/05/23/80319391.html.

THE NEW YORK TIMES. "In Pasteur's Laboratory." *The New York Times*, 22 Dec. 1885, timesmachine.nytimes.com/timesmachine/1885/12/22/103646754.html.

THE NEW YORK TIMES. "Influenza Vaccine Perfected in War." *The New York Times*, 9 Mar. 1946, timesmachine.nytimes.com/timesmachine/1946/03/09/100995291.html.

THE NEW YORK TIMES. "Lister's War on Pain and Death." *The New York Times*, 18 Feb. 1912, https://timesmachine.nytimes.com/timesmachine/1912/02/18/100352215.html.

THE NEW YORK TIMES. "Medical." *The New York Times*, 17 Mar. 1854, timesmachine.nytimes.com/timesmachine/1854/03/17/75366047.html.

THE NEW YORK TIMES. "Microbes Caught in Action." *The New York Times*, 31 Oct. 1909, https://timesmachine.nytimes.com/timesmachine/1909/10/31/106778062.html.

THE NEW YORK TIMES. "Modern Wound Treatment." *The New York Times*, 10 June 1894, timesmachine.nytimes.com/timesmachine/1894/06/10/106099210.html.

THE NEW YORK TIMES. "Nation's Death Rate Halved Since 1900." *The New York Times*, 6 July 1930, timesmachine.nytimes.com/timesmachine/1930/07/06/96907936.html.

THE NEW YORK TIMES. "A New Anaesthetic Process." *The New York Times*, 1 Apr. 1866, https://timesmachine.nytimes.com/timesmachine/1866/04/01/83452978.html.

THE NEW YORK TIMES. "New Device Records Action of the Heart." *The New York Times*, 19 Nov. 1924, https://timesmachine.nytimes.com /timesmachine/1924/11/19/105467497.html.

THE NEW YORK TIMES. "New Discoveries May Eliminate Quinine for Malaria." *The New York Times*, 13 July 1913, https://timesmachine.nytimes.com /timesmachine/1913/07/13/100635307.html.

THE NEW YORK TIMES. "New Drug Is Used to Treat Typhoid." *The New York Times*, 24 May 1945, timesmachine.nytimes.com/timesmachine/1945/05 /24/88233332.html.

THE NEW YORK TIMES. "The Phipps Psychiatric Clinic." *The New York Times*, 25 June 1908, https://timesmachine.nytimes.com/timesmachine/1908 /06/25/105007146.html.

THE NEW YORK TIMES. "Prosthetic Limbs, Controlled by Thought." *The New York Times*, 19 Jan. 2018, www.nytimes.com/2015/05/21/technology/a -bionic-approach-to-prosthetics-controlled-by-thought.html.

THE NEW YORK TIMES. "The Roentgen Discovery." *The New York Times*, 7 Feb. 1896, timesmachine.nytimes.com/timesmachine/1896/02/07/104110602.html.

THE NEW YORK TIMES. "Serum Discovered for Scarlet Fever by Long Research." *The New York Times*, 17 Jan. 1924, https://timesmachine .nytimes.com/timesmachine/1924/01/17/101577707.html.

THE NEW YORK TIMES. "Serum Proves Boon in Fighting Diabetes." *The New York Times*, 8 Oct. 1922, https://timesmachine.nytimes.com/timesmachine /1922/10/08/107071266.html.

THE NEW YORK TIMES. "Substitute for Anesthesia." *The New York Times*, 4 Jan. 1860, timesmachine.nytimes.com/timesmachine/1860/01/04/83207706.html.

THE NEW YORK TIMES. "The Triumphs of Surgery." *The New York Times*, 10 Oct. 1897, timesmachine.nytimes.com/timesmachine/1897/10/10/105954961.html.

THE NEW YORK TIMES. "Vaccination Against Cholera." *The New York Times*, 9 May 1893, timesmachine.nytimes.com/timesmachine/1893/05/09 /106823482.html.

THE NEW YORK TIMES. "Vaccine Is Found for Yellow Fever." *The New York Times*, 23 Mar. 1938, timesmachine.nytimes.com/timesmachine/1938 /03/23/96808675.html.

THE NEW YORK TIMES. "Woman Gives Birth to Baby Conceived Outside the Body." *The New York Times*, 26 July 1978, www.nytimes.com/1978/07/26 /archives/new-jersey-pages-woman-gives-birth-to-baby-conceived -outside-the.html.

NORTH AMERICAN NEWSPAPER ALLIANCE. "Known Viruses Now Exceed 300." *The New York Times*, 7 Dec. 1958, timesmachine.nytimes.com /timesmachine/1958/12/07/93611040.html.

THE PALL MALL GAZETTE. "A Cure for Snakebite." *The New York Times*, 27 Mar. 1898, timesmachine.nytimes.com/timesmachine/1898/03/27/102108879.html.

POLLACK, ANDREW. "Cloning Is Used to Create Embryonic Stem Cells." *The New York Times,* 19 Oct. 2018, www.nytimes.com/2013/05/16/science /scientists-use-cloning-to-create-embryonic-stem-cells.html.

SCHMECK, HAROLD M., JR. "Body's Rejection of Heart Feared." *The New York Times*, 4 Dec. 1967, timesmachine.nytimes.com/timesmachine/1967/12 /04/93878867.html.

SCHMECK, HAROLD M., JR. "A Mumps Vaccine Is Licensed by U.S." *The New York Times*, 5 Jan. 1968, timesmachine.nytimes.com/timesmachine/1968 /01/05/91219610.html.

SCHMECK, HAROLD M., JR. "Vaccines Hailed as Measles Doom." *The New York Times*, 11 Feb. 1965, timesmachine.nytimes.com/timesmachine/1965/02/11 /95530731.html.

SULLIVAN, RONALD. "New Procedure Aids Some Heart Patients." *The New York Times*, 17 June 1978, www.nytimes.com/1978/06/17/archives/new -procedure-aids-some-heart-patients-opens-clogged-arteries-by.html.

SULLIVAN, WALTER. "Pregnancy Lab Reports a Success." *The New York Times*, 12 May 1981, www.nytimes.com/1981/05/12/science/pregnancy-lab-reports -a-success.html.

THORNE, VAN BUREN, M.D. "Typhus, War's Dread Ally, Beaten." *The New York Times*, 18 Apr. 1915, https://timesmachine.nytimes.com/timesmachine/1915 /04/18/100150831.html.

UGWU, REGGIE. "Veterans Groups Push for Medical Marijuana to Treat PTSD." *The New York Times*, 4 Nov. 2017, www.nytimes.com/2017/11/03/us /medical-marijuana-veterans.html.

WADE, NICHOLAS. "Once Again, Scientists Say Human Genome Is Complete." *The New York Times*, 15 Apr. 2003, www.nytimes.com/2003/04/15/science /once-again-scientists-say-human-genome-is-complete.html.

Index

This book is current up until the time of printing. For the most up-to-date reporting, visit www.nytimes.com.